The Great German Mystics

ECKHART, TAULER

AND

SUSO

James M. Clark

Dover Publications, Inc.
Mineola, New York

Bibliographical Note

This Dover edition, first published in 2013, is an unabridged republication of the work originally published in 1949 by Basil Blackwell and Mott, Ltd., London.

International Standard Book Number

ISBN-13: 978-0-486-44734-6
ISBN-10: 0-486-44734-0

Manufactured in the United States by Courier Corporation
44734001
www.doverpublications.com

PREFACE

IN order to keep this book within reasonable dimensions, it seemed desirable to restrict the field to the Middle Ages and to writings in the vernacular. Angelus Silesius and Jacob Böhme are excluded by the first condition, and Thomas à Kempis by the second. As the fifteenth century is a period of decadence, we are concerned almost entirely with the fourteenth. The limits proposed make the subject compact and homogeneous. Some reference to the Latin literature of the time is, of course, unavoidable, but it is merely incidental. The method of treatment is determined by the nature of the subject. When dealing with Eckhart, Tauler, Suso and Merswin, the ascertained facts must be disentangled from a mass of legend and fiction. In the sphere of Franciscan mysticism new ground has to be broken and unpublished material sifted.

When I first became interested in German mystics I derived much stimulus from talks with the late J. G. Sikes of Cambridge, whose knowledge of Eckhart and his background was as accurate as it was extensive. Professor W. G. Maclagan of Glasgow University, very kindly read through part of my manuscript and made some valuable comments. I am indebted to Professor R. Klibansky for useful information on points of detail. The work could not have been completed so soon if it were not for the fact that the University of Glasgow gave me leave of absence during the Easter Term of 1948 and also a grant towards travelling expenses. For this my grateful thanks are due, and no less to the Carnegie Trust for the Universities of Scotland for a generous contribution towards the cost of publishing this book. I should like to take this opportunity of thanking Dr. F. Burckhardt, Director of the Zentralbibliothek, Zurich, and Professor Forrer of Zurich, Dr. Karl Schwarber, Director of the University Library, and Dr. Burckhardt of the Department of Manuscripts at Basel, and finally the staff of Glasgow University Library, for much kindness and helpfulness.

J. M. C.

October, 1948

CONTENTS

THE GREAT GERMAN MYSTICS

CHAPTER I

INTRODUCTION

THE mystical movement of the fourteenth century in Germany was a remarkable, perhaps a unique, phenomenon in the history of mediaeval culture. It included three major writers: Eckhart, Tauler and Suso, and a host of others of lesser rank. What is more, it produced a reading public for their voluminous works. For the vast number of mystical sermons, tractates and anecdotes that were written in the vernacular at this time presupposes a large reading public. The latter were not confined to conventuals: communities of pious layfolk were also affected. Both in quality and in quantity the literary production is amazing: Eckhart and his compeers belong to the greatest mystics of all time. There has been much speculation as to the cause. How does it come about that at this particular time and in this particular country this phenomenon should have occurred?

It was a time of crisis, of violent upheavals in church and state, of bitter conflict. It began with the downfall of the powerful Hohenstaufen dynasty and the Great Interregnum (1250–1272). It continued through the 'Babylonian Captivity' of the papacy at Avignon and the struggle between the Pope and the Emperor from 1317 to 1347. This phase closed with the death of Ludwig the Bavarian in 1347. Civil war, anarchy, ban and interdict were followed by awe-inspiring natural calamities: pestilence, famine, earthquakes, and floods. The natural result of all this was to create a deep sense of the insecurity of human life and the evanescence of human happiness. The impending end of the world was a common theme in this troubled time.

Does this sombre background of crimes and calamities sufficiently explain the great diffusion of mystical experience and mystical literature in the Empire between about 1250 and 1370? Are we to consider that the temporal weakness of the Church, the exile of the Holy See, the undeniable corruption of morals in clergy and laity alike, caused the finer spirits of the age to take refuge in a spiritual religion, freed from the shackles of dogma and authority? Many writers answer this question in the affirmative. Was not Vienna the musical centre of Europe when Austria lay prostrate under the heel of Napoleon? Were not the Germans a nation of poets and philosophers at the time when their political fortunes were at their lowest ebb? Can we infer that like music and literature, mysticism is the product of political disintegration and material chaos?

There is much to be said against this hypothesis. Spanish mysticism flourished not at a time of decline, but in the greatest age of Spain, the sixteenth century, when her power and culture were at their zenith. Moreover, there have been other periods in European history that were equally catastrophic without being productive in the religious field. Italy had anarchy and civil wars in plenty and the Black Death into the bargain, but they produced nothing parallel to the mystical movement in Germany. It is, therefore, difficult to believe that adverse conditions are essential to the growth of mysticism. Nevertheless, one might concede the point that about the middle of the fourteenth century the historical background is reflected in the works of the German mystics. But this would not apply to earlier writers and least of all to Eckhart, the greatest of them all.

According to another theory, the movement of mysticism is a reaction against the sterile discussions of the schools, the cold abstractions of theologians. This is a one-sided and superficial view. We cannot get over the fact that Eckhart himself was a product of scholasticism, a typical representative of metaphysical speculation. So far from rebelling against these traditions, he accepted them implicitly in all their main tenets. Never is he found in opposition to Thomas Aquinas or Albertus Magnus in an essential point of doctrine. He did not dislike syllogistic reasoning or even juggling with words. He was himself an arch-juggler. He did not object to theology, but considered it of supreme importance. Of all mystics of the post-classical era Eckhart is the most intellectual.

It is true that one must draw a distinction between the period up to 1328 and that which follows. After the death of Eckhart mysticism ceased to be speculative and became practical. This was due in some measure to the trial and condemnation of Eckhart, but there were other causes. Later Dominican writers were inferior in intellectual capacity or were too much occupied with other matters to devote themselves to philosophical problems. It has also been suggested that the victorious advance of Nominalism undermined confidence in human reason, allowed the will to take the place ·of the intellect as the highest human faculty and put ethics in the fore-front instead of metaphysics.[1]

---

[1] Josef Quint, in *Reallexikon der deutschen Literaturgeschichte*, Berlin, 1931, IV, 82–83.

Whatever the cause, it is certain that learning was discredited by Tauler and his contemporaries. They refer to reason in disparaging terms; the word 'master' often has a derogatory sound. Of the three stages of the mystic way: purgative, illuminative and unitive, it is now the first two, the preparatory stages, that are commended and explored, the final one recedes in importance.

Are we justified in regarding German mysticism as a kind of protest against institutional religion? The real leaders of the movement were priests and hence members of the hierarchy. They had no reason for rebellion against the established order, nor were they rebels by nature. The search for inner perfection meant more to them than the machinery of administration. As for the free congregations of women, that is to say the houses of Beguines or the groups known as Friends of God, they were not instituted in opposition to the Church as it then existed. In their origins they were a result of the conditions of the times and were, so to speak, a by-product of monasticism. The Beguines were candidates for the cloister who could not be admitted for pecuniary or other reasons. They had no grievance against organized religion and wished for nothing better than to be nuns in a regular order. If they, or some of them, later developed on particular lines and even acquired heretical opinions, that was in no way connected with their origins, but was due to other causes.

As a result of continual wars, tournaments and jousts, there were heavy casualties among the male population, particularly the nobles, and a surplus of women. The influence of the Crusades in this respect, as in so many others, has often been exaggerated. They were only one of several factors. Many of the unmarried women tended to enter convents, which increased as a result in size and importance. In Strasbourg alone there were six Dominican nunneries in the early fourteenth century. There were eight in the district of Constance. In 1303 there were only fourteen in the whole of France.[1]

Although the convents were so numerous, they were unable to cope with the applications for admission. The recognized orders could only found a new house or adopt an existing one under certain conditions. Official sanction usually required the intervention of an influential personage with the authorities. A convent had to be financially independent and free of the necessity of raising further funds. This meant a rich founder or wealthy inmates who could bring with them a dowry that would yield a substantial annuity. Hence the

---

[1] R. P. Mortier, *Histoire abrégé de l'Ordre de Saint-Dominique*, Tours, 1920, p. 75.

majority of the nuns were women of high rank, nobles, or patricians from the growing towns. Many of them were highly educated and knew Latin. Thus it came about that in the crowded Dominican nunneries there was an active intellectual life. We come across nuns who wrote original works in prose or verse and some who translated Latin passages into German.

If German mysticism can be explained at all, the true explanation is that of Denifle,[1] who connects it with two things: first the obligation imposed on the Dominican friars to supervise the nunneries of their Order, and secondly the reform of Dominican convents of nuns in Germany about 1286-7. In 1245 the Friars Preachers took over the pastoral care of Dominican nunneries in Germany, which included the hearing of confessions, administration of the sacraments, preaching and regular visitation. There were also heavy administrative duties involved. The nunneries benefited considerably because they enjoyed all the privileges of the Order and were protected against encroachments. As a result of regular supervision the discipline was maintained and the spiritual life of the convents was guarded against aberrations of all kinds.

There were, however, grave disadvantages for the friars. Those selected to undertake the pastoral care of nunneries were above all the learned brethren, the *magistri* and lectors. They found themselves unable to pursue their studies because of the perpetual interruptions. The rapid growth of the nunneries made it an ever increasing burden. In the Province of Theutonia there were some seventy at the beginning of the fourteenth century. In the whole of Europe, including the Province of Saxony, the Order had only about ninety converts of nuns. In Theutonia there were between forty-six and forty-eight friaries, and hence the latter were far outnumbered by the nunneries. Elsewhere the opposite was the case. In addition to the regular convents there were the houses of Beguines which needed careful supervision. Obviously the task of the learned friars was extremely onerous.

The Dominicans made repeated efforts to be released from their obligations in this direction, and in 1252 Innocent IV yielded to their solicitations. In view of the fact that they were impeded by their new duties in the performance of their main task, which was that of preaching, he exempted them from the care of nunneries, excepting those of St. Sisto in Rome and Prouille in the South of France, which had been founded by St. Dominic himself. Two years later the Pope rescinded the provisions of the Bull and instructed Cardinal Hugo de

[1] *Archiv*, II, 641. See also Grundmann, *Religiöse Bewegungen*, 274-304, Berlin, 1935.

Cher to make out new regulations. In 1256 the German Provincial was ordered to take over responsibility for all the Dominican nunneries in his province, and in the following year, the General Chapter of Florence extended this obligation to include all nunneries that had been previously in possession of this privilege, that is to say, nunneries of other orders. This state of affairs continued practically unchanged till the Council of Trent.

The growth of mysticism was then due to the impact of scholastic philosophy on educated women in nunneries. The friars had to express theological and philosophical ideas in a garb that would make them intelligible to women. The nuns stimulated the pastoral work of the friars and the friars encouraged the nuns to press on in the search for spiritual perfection. Mechthild von Magdeburg heard sermons preached by the friars and she had a Dominican as her confessor. He encouraged her to write and assisted her in so doing. Suso's friend, Elsbeth Stagel, secretly wrote down what Suso had told her by word of mouth or by letter about his own life. She was his Egeira and no doubt inspired some of his noblest utterances. Adelheid Langmann cured a man in Nürnberg of suicidal mania as a result of her intercessions. He became an Austin friar and studied in Paris. Heinrich von Nördlingen corresponded with Margareta Ebner at Medingen and ascribed great importance to her visions and revelations.

Many of the finest mystical writings are sermons preached to nuns. Most of Tauler's sermons belong to this category. Many nuns wrote down afterwards what they had heard the preacher say in the pulpit and some of them had quite phenomenal memories. The preachers themselves sometimes wrote down their own sermons or composed treatises of a devotional nature in the vernacular. Scholasticism provided a philosophy of mysticism. The stages of the way that led towards union with God were mapped out and described. All this was in Latin. To make it intelligible to laymen or nuns it had to be translated into German. The technical terms were lacking; they had to be improvised. After passing through the crucible of translation, the thought was imperceptibly changed. It was simplified, and one might say coloured, both by the preacher and his congregation. There was a marked preference for certain Biblical passages: the opening words of St. John's Gospel, the Song of Songs considered as an allegory of the love for Christ and His Church, the scene of Paul's conversion on the road to Damascus and his account of what then happened.

If we compare Eckhart's Latin works which are so learned and at times so abstruse, with his German sermons, we see the effect of preaching to women. The learned tone becomes popular and homely. The enthusiasms which are restrained in the Latin treatises, burst forth freely. Abstractions tend to disappear and everything becomes more concrete and simple. There is more of the personal note. Here and there the preacher speaks in the first person to bring some point home. He introduces a vivid piece of dialogue, using the dramatic form to enliven his discourse. He is not now using the language of the learned, but his own mother tongue, and using it as it had seldom been used before.

It is a mistake to consider that German mysticism begins and ends with the three great names of Eckhart, Tauler and Suso. Certainly these giants tend to dwarf their contemporaries, but their predecessors were by no means a negligible quantity, if inferior to them in intellect and literary power. Later writers preserve the traditions of the past without notably enriching or extending them. There were minor mystics, chiefly Dominicans, such as Eckhart the Younger, Eckhart Rube, Franke and others. Very little of their work has been preserved: we have only a few odd sermons and sayings by them. As far as we can judge from the scanty material available, these writers are either contemporaries of Eckhart and kindred spirits, or they belong to an orthodox Thomist section without that strong strain of Neo-Platonism that distinguishes Eckhart and his disciples. One hesitates to speak of a school of Eckhart, because of the paucity of evidence, but there are excellent reasons for thinking that Tauler and Suso were by no means the only gifted pupils of the master, and that his fervid eloquence kindled a flame that long survived his condemnation and death.

It is customary to regard German mysticism as an entirely Dominican product and to ignore or minimize the Franciscan contribution. A reassessment is therefore necessary. David von Augsburg died about the time when Eckhart was born. Most of his works are in Latin, but his German prose is remarkable for its clarity and beauty. The greatest of Franciscan mystics is Marquart von Lindau, who kept alive in a dull and prosaic age the spirit of his predecessors.

CHAPTER II

ECKHART

ECKHART was born about 1260 at Hochheim, two miles north of Gotha, and was therefore, like Luther, a native of Thuringia. There is no foundation for the legend, first recorded in the sixteenth century, that he was born in Strasbourg. He was of noble birth, an Eckhart of Hochheim is mentioned in a charter dated 1251.[1] In 1305 a knight named 'Eckhardus de Hochheim,' who owned property in the neighbourhood of Gotha, transferred a plot of land to the Cistercian nuns of that town. Among the witnesses who signed the document was 'the venerable Friar, Magister Eckhardus of Paris, Provincial of the Order of Preachers in the Province of Saxony,'[2] This witness was no other than our Eckhart; he was the kinsman, probably the son, of the knight.

In the last quarter of the thirteenth century the Dominican Order was at the very height of its fame, and in Germany, as elsewhere, many youths of high rank and intellectual ability were attracted to it. Eckhart was among them and he became a novice at the nearest convent, which was that of Erfurt. Entrants to the Order had to be at least fifteen years of age and they were expected to have attained at least a competent knowledge of Latin, but this latter rule was not always rigidly enforced. After the preliminary course of instruction was completed, it was customary to send promising young friars from Erfurt to the *studium generale* at Cologne to study theology. It is highly probable that Eckhart studied in that city. His works show a close acquaintance with the writings of Albertus Magnus and Thomas Aquinas, who had raised the reputation of the Cologne school to its highest point. But as St. Thomas Aquinas died in 1274 and Albertus in 1280, it is unlikely for chronological reasons that Eckhart knew either of these two great scholars personally.

Towards the end of the thirteenth century he was in Erfurt once more and was elected by his brethren as their prior.[3] About the year 1300 he was sent to Paris, first to learn and then to teach. It may seem strange that a friar who had been so highly honoured by his own

[1] *Thuringia Sacra*, Frankofurti, 1737, p. 486.
[2] Denifle, *Die Heimat Meister Eckeharts*, p. 355.
[3] Quétif-Echard, *Scriptores Ordines Praedicatorum*, I, 507.

7

convent should be relieved of his post in order to continue his studies. But it was by no means unusual for a friar to serve for a short time in the administration of the Order or in a teaching capacity before going to Paris, which was the centre of the educational system of the Dominicans. It was a high distinction to be chosen to go to the *studium generale* ât Saint-Jacques in Paris; only three students from each province enjoyed this privilege. The course consisted normally of five years of theological study before the degree of Baccalaureus was taken. Then came three years' teaching under the direction of the Magister. At the age of thirty-five, or earlier if special dispensation was given, the candidate was presented to the Chancellor to receive the licentiate, which entitled him to teach as magister or doctor. Those who graduated at Paris in this way as Doctors of Theology (*magistri in sacra pagina*) formed the intellectual *élite* of the Western Church. Evidently in Eckhart's case the course of instruction was considerably reduced.

In an old history of the Dominican Order it is stated that in 1302 'Frater Aychardus Theutonicus' obtained the licentiate in Paris.[1] The doctorate was conferred upon him by Boniface, but it is unlikely that, as some have thought, the degree was conferred by the Pope in person or that Eckhart had to go to Rome to receive it. It should be remembered that a bitter struggle was going on between Louis-Phillipe of France and the papacy. The Dominicans were loyal to the Pope, while the University of Paris supported the King. Direct papal intervention was needed to secure the doctorate of Paris for Dominican Friars. The fact that Eckhart received the licentiate presupposes that he had lectured on the *Sentences* in Paris for at least a year as *Baccalaureus*, that is to say, that he had lectured on Aristotelian philosophy, as understood and expounded in the Middle Ages. This was confirmed by the discovery of some fragments of Eckhart's earliest known work, a commentary on the first four books of the *Sentences*,[2] written between 1300 and 1302.

The disputes between scholars, to which the outside public was admitted, were a well-known feature of the University of Paris. Eckhart was selected to defend the doctrines of his Order: a high distinction reserved for the ablest of scholars only. Two treatises have been preserved in which we see him engaged in vigorous controversy with a Franciscan friar.

From Paris Eckhart was recalled home to take part in administrative work. Germany formed originally one Dominican province, but it

[1] Denifle, *Archiv*, II, p. 211.   [2] *Glorieux*, p. 180.

had now been divided into two: Saxony and Alemannia. Erfurt belonged to the former, and in 1303, at the Erfurt Chapter, Eckhart was appointed Provincial Minister of Saxony. On the expiration of this charge he was made Vicar General of Bohemia with full powers. He was thus entrusted with the difficult task of carrying through a reform of the Dominican convents of Bohemia. It has been suggested that his recall was due to his leniency towards the Brethren of the Free Spirit, a heretical sect that was widely spread in Bohemia, but there is no evidence for this.

At this time Eckhart was unquestionably one of the most eminent and respected members of his Order in Germany. His fame was not confined to his own native province of Saxony; he was also honourably known in the much larger and more important province of Alemannia, which included all the rest of Germany. In 1310 he was elected Provincial Minister of this vast and populous region, but the election was not confirmed by the General Chapter of Naples, apparently because a recent regulation forbade friars to hold administrative office outside their native province. Being thus unable to act as Provincial, he was sent to Paris to lecture at the *studium generale*. During this second stay (1311–12), he once more took part in public disputations with the Franciscans and among his Latin works we find three *Quaestiones* which represent his contribution to a controversy with a Minorite named Gonsalvus.[1]

Eckhart's stay in the French capital was of short duration. The next recorded fact in his life is his presence in Strasbourg in 1314;[2] he was apparently a lector in the Dominican convent. It was during this period that he preached to nuns and layfolk with such acceptance that he soon became the most popular preacher in Germany. Strasbourg was a great centre of religious life in the fourteenth century. In the pulpits of the cathedral and the numerous religious houses of the city great orators were to be heard. In the nunneries mysticism was cultivated with ardent zeal. There were besides the religious congregations, communities of pious laymen and women who although not tied by formal vows, devoted themselves to the practice of religion and good works. Eckhart's name is very closely associated with Strasbourg and this is no doubt the reason for the tradition, already mentioned, that he was a native of the place. Nowhere else had he so many devoted disciples, nowhere else was his name so highly honoured and his memory so faithfully preserved.

---

[1] A. Dondaine, *Magistri Eckardi Opera Latina*, p. xi.   [2] Denifle, *Archiv*, II, 211.

But there are very few certain facts about this period of his life and the recorded traditions must be scrutinized carefully.

There is a gap in our information between the years 1314 and 1326, but a recent discovery throws some light on this obscure period.[1] There had been a dispute between the Teutonic Knights and the Dominicans of Mulhouse (Mühlhausen) in Alsace. A charter dated 1319, now in the archives of Mulhouse, indicates that the quarrel had been settled. The document is signed by Hartung, the Provincial Prior of Saxony, and Eckhart. The latter is designated as Vicar, and as his signature comes first, this leads to the conclusion that Eckhart was at this time Vicar General of the Province of Saxony. This at least is certain, Eckhart was in Mulhouse in 1319 and took part in the settlement of the local dispute.

Charles Schmid, and other writers after him, thought that Eckhart was in touch with the heretical Beghards at Strasbourg, but this is pure conjecture and is highly improbable. Eckhart's assertion before his judges on January 24, 1327, that no friar of his Order in Germany had ever been accused of heresy, rings true and was not contradicted by his accusers. A good deal of misunderstanding has been caused by a letter written by Herveus, General of the Dominican Order, to the priors of Worms and Mainz, relating to grave offences alleged against 'Friar Ekardus, our prior in Frankfort and Friar Theoderichus of St. Martin, suspected of evil communications.' It was ordered that an investigation should be made and the accused punished if found guilty. This passage led Preger and many subsequent writers to assume, first that Meister Eckhart was prior of Frankfort, secondly that he had associated with heretics, thirdly that he was convicted and punished for this offence. All these assumptions are false. Our Eckhart was never prior of Frankfort and was not qualified to act as such, since he was a native of the Saxon province. The similarity of names is a mere coincidence. There were at least three well-known friars called Eckhart in the Dominican Order at this time in Germany.[2] Moreover, our friar is usually called 'Magister Eckhardus.' The phrase 'suspecta familiaritas' is used, as Denifle has shown,[3] in the sense of improper familiarity with women and never of association with heretics. It is also impossible to believe that a man convicted of so serious an offence would be immediately afterwards sent to the leading educational centre of the Order of Preachers in the Empire, there to lecture as senior professor.

[1] E. Schröder, in *Anzeiger für deutsches Altertum*, 55 (1936), pp. 216–217.
[2] See Spamer, *Überlieferung der Eckeharttexte*, p. 396.   [3] *Archiv*, II, 618–624.

He enjoyed an excellent reputation: of this there is abundant evidence. He is frequently referred to by contemporaries as 'holy master' or 'saintly man.' Never is there the slightest suggestion that his conduct was other than exemplary.

There is no documentary evidence to show that Eckhart had dealings with heretics at Strasbourg. On the other hand it is quite possible that in this period he came under suspicion of dealing in his sermons with abstruse matters which the common people could not understand. His words were written down by members of his congregation and were distorted and thus liable to misinterpretation. At the General Chapter in Venice in 1325 complaints had been made of certain German friars who preached about subtle and lofty matters to the people to the peril of their souls. It is by no means certain that these strictures were directed against Eckhart. Other delicate topics were in the air at the time, such as the quarrel between Ludwig the Bavarian and the Pope and the reference may be to them.

This is, however, not an isolated complaint. In Strasbourg itself the same accusation was made and this time directly against Eckhart. A Strasbourg devotional writer named Rulmann Merswin,[1] of whom we shall have more to say in a later chapter, tells us that a devout priest called on Meister Eckhart, to give him a friendly warning about his sermons, urging him to give up preaching of matters that very few people could understand or profit by and to consider Christ's preaching and teaching, which was directed to the call to repentance, to desist from evil and to do good. The only authority for this anecdote was Merswin, who was not a very reliable witness; the whole story may be apocryphal, but it seems to reflect the views of some sections of the public at the time.[2]

In the final phase of his career he was the senior lector at the Dominican *studium generale* of Cologne. But he was not destined to end his days in peace. In 1326 he was summoned before the archiepiscopal court to answer a charge of heresy. The remainder of his life was clouded by the trial but before the final verdict was passed Eckhart had died. Most modern authorities assign his death to the year 1327, but without sufficient reason. All that we know is he died between 1327 and 1329. A phrase in the papal bull of 1329 suggests that his death was then quite recent.

It was apparently as a result of the complaints made at Venice in 1325, and with the approval of the Order that the Pope appointed

---

[1] Jundt, *Essai sur le mysticisme populaire*, pp. 215–221.
[2] See also Grabmann, *Neue Eckhartforschungen*, p. 78.

Nicholas of Strasbourg, a Dominican friar and lector in the Cologne *studium generale*, as inquisitor of the Province of Germany, to inquire into and correct faith and morals. The new inquisitor examined Eckhart and exonerated him of guilt in July, 1326. At this point the Archbishop of Cologne opened proceedings against Eckhart. In the course of the process he called upon Nicholas of Strasbourg to communicate to him the findings of his court. Instead of doing so, Nicholas proceeded to the court to enter a formal protest on January 13, 1327.[1] He denounced the charges against Eckhart as calumnious and false, accused the Archbishop of acting without sufficiently hearing the other side, and moreover of acting illegally. He challenged the right of the Archbishop to summon him, Nicholas, before his tribunal. By virtue of the papal mandate conferred upon him Nicholas was inquisitor of the Province of Germany, and to question his authority was derogatory to the authority of the Pope. Quite apart from this, the Dominicans alone were competent in the matter, since the Church had entrusted them with full powers to investigate cases of alleged heresy. After elaborating these points, he appealed to the Pope. Nicholas repeated his protests, but the Archbishop took no notice of them and summoned Eckhart to appear before him.

Thanks to the investigations of Preger, Denifle, Théry and others and the discovery of new documents, it is now possible to reconstruct the trial stage by stage. A list of forty-nine articles purporting to be drawn from his writings or his sermons was presented to Eckhart on September 26, 1326, by the Inquisitors. He made a written reply. Expressing himself in firm, but courteous terms, he refused to acknowledge the competency of the court, asserting that as a Dominican he was not subject to the authority of the Archbishop. The Dominicans were responsible only to the Pope. He accused the Inquisitors of dilatory procedure. He urged that two of the witnesses who testified against him were men of his own Order who were notoriously immoral. Eckhart also claimed that there were irregularities in the accusation itself; he complained of false allegations and stoutly protested his innocence. Finally he appealed to the Pope.

Then the accusers returned to the attack. A new list of fifty-nine articles, more detailed than the first, was placed before him and again he replied at some length. On January 24, 1327 Eckhart appealed directly to the Pope. The appeal was rejected by the Inquisitors as 'irrelevant.' Feeling that he had been basely calumniated and that his

[1] Preger, *Meister Eckhart und die Inquisition*, pp. 29–31.

Order was also involved in the scandal, feeling in fact that it was the Order that was being attacked through him, Eckhart made a public declaration in the Dominican Church of Cologne on February 13, 1327. After the sermon he called upon another friar, named Conrad von Halberstadt, to read aloud a Latin statement from a scroll in his hand. Eckhart translated it sentence by sentence into the vulgar tongue. He affirmed in the presence of a large congregation and of several members of his Order that he had always abhorred all errors of faith and aberrations in morals. Further he retracted in advance any error that might be found in his writings or sayings.

Eckhart's appeal had been dismissed, but the trial had attracted attention elsewhere and the papal curia ordered that all documents should be sent to Avignon, where the trial was reopened. It has been asserted that at Avignon Eckhart's writings were examined and new propositions were taken from them, chiefly from the *Commentary on the Gospel of St. John*, but this view seems to be erroneous.[1] As Eckhart had admitted that a number of the suspect passages were to be found in his written works or had been used in his sermons, the papal curia only considered the question whether these passages were orthodox or not.

In 1329 Pope John XXII issued a Bull, entitled *In Agro Dominico*, in which twenty-eight propositions were condemned, seventeen of them as heretical and eleven as dangerous or suspect. On April 5th the Pope ordered the Archbishop of Cologne to publish the Bull in his diocese together with the condemned articles, lest Eckhart's errors 'should take deeper root in the hearts of those simple-minded persons to whom he had preached.' It was also stated in the Bull that before his death Eckhart had retracted twenty-six of the articles in question and everything which was capable of leading to error in his works 'as far as it can be so understood.' He submitted formally to the authority of the Apostolic See. As he had declared before the Inquisition, he was 'capable of error, but not of heresy, because the one depends on the understanding, the other on the will.'

We know that Eckhart went to Avignon to defend his convictions in person; the evidence is provided by a passage in William Ockham's *Dialogus*.[2] Ockham was in a position to know because he himself was tried at Avignon and moreover by Cardinal Fournier, who was one of the judges of Eckhart. We are told that 'A certain Master of Theology of the Dominican Order, Aycardus Theutonicus,' taught many absurd things. Ockham gives a sample by quoting five of the

---

[1] Pelster, *Ein Gutachten*.   [2] See *Alois Dempf*, p. 84.

alleged doctrines of Eckhart and then proceeds, 'First he was accused in the Court of the Archbishop of Cologne ... later he went to Avignon; his judges were appointed and he did not deny that he had taught and preached the aforesaid doctrines. He was not convicted, nor were the propositions already cited and others immediately condemned, but they were handed over to the Cardinals to determine whether they were to be considered heretical. Also some Masters of Theology were commissioned to investigate them.'[1]

It seems remarkable that a man who had held high office in the Order of Preachers, who had been entrusted with the education of young friars and the pastoral care of nuns, should have been accused of false doctrine. Did not the Dominicans pride themselves on their strict orthodoxy? Was not the Order founded for the express purpose of combating heresy? It is still more remarkable that Eckhart should have been found guilty of the charges brought against him. Did he receive a fair trial? The question has been answered differently. It was the subject of violent controversy in his day and has been hotly debated in our own.

Let us deal first with the Cologne process. It is clear that the Ordinary, in this case the Archbishop of Cologne, was the proper authority to deal with matters of faith and doctrine in his diocese. Whether a Dominican friar was subject to his jurisdiction was a debatable point.[2] Inquisitors, whether papal or episcopal, were entitled to examine members of all religious bodies. But the Dominicans claimed exemption by virtue of special immunity granted them by the Pope. Where canon law was ambiguous, they appealed to common law in their support. Apart from this question, and here at least there was room for doubt, the trial observed the forms of law. Definite charges were made against Eckhart; they were substantiated by quotations from his sermons and books. The accusation was presented in writing. The accused was given the aid of two imperial public notaries to put the documents in proper legal form. He had the opportunity of preparing his defence and answering the charges point by point.

When all this has been conceded it must be admitted that the documents do not give us the impression of judicial impartiality. One suspects the desire to get an adverse verdict rather than the desire to get at the true facts of the case. Sentences were reported from sermons; was this evidence or mere hearsay? Is it credible

---

[1] In Goldast, *Monarchiæ S. Romani Imperii*, Francofordi, 1614, t. II, p. 909.
[2] H. C. Lea, *A History of the Inquisition in the Middle Ages*, London, 1888, pp. 361–363.

that Eckhart had openly said that his little finger had created the universe? The friar himself strenuously denied it in the presence of his own congregation in his own church, explaining the charge as being perhaps due to a passage in which he was speaking of the Infant Jesus. At Avignon this particular article is not mentioned at all. What was the motive behind the trial? Let us consider some of the personalities who were involved.

Heinrich von Firneburg, Archbishop of Cologne, who presided over the court, had the reputation of being a stern man. During his tenure of office scores of Beghards were handed over to the secular arm.[1] He was, moreover, a partisan of Ludwig the Bavarian, and hence belonged to the anti-papal party in Germany. He had, therefore, no tenderness for the Dominicans, whose fidelity to the papacy was well-known. A dispassionate verdict could scarcely be expected from him. Among the witnesses we notice the names of two Franciscan friars, Magister Reyner and Friar Albert of Cologne, who testified against Eckhart. Here we have a clue to the origin of the process.

The two great Mendicant Orders had a great deal in common and the relations between them were as a rule cordial, but at this particular time and place there was unconcealed hostility between them. The long dispute about realism and nominalism had divided Dominicans and Franciscans and now a new grievance embittered their relationship. The canonization of Thomas Aquinas was felt to be a Dominican victory; his doctrines were officially adopted by the Church and the Franciscans had to submit. They took their revenge by striking at Eckhart, the outstanding Dominican in Germany, and striking him where they knew him to be vulnerable. It cannot be denied that the Franciscans bore the chief responsibility of the proceedings at Cologne.[2]

The attitude of some Franciscans towards Eckhart may be judged by a document expressing the views of four turbulent friars, of whom William Ockham was one.[3] They protested against the 'detestable heresies' of Eckhart and criticized the Pope for taking no action in the matter. This was in 1328, immediately before the opening of the Avignon process. Incidentally, this was not the only bone of contention between the 'Spiritual' Franciscans and John XXII. They denounced his views on the question of the poverty of Christ and

[1] Johannes Vitoduranus, *Chronicon*, p. 36 (in *Thesaurus Historiæ Helveticæ*, Tiguri, 1735).
[2] Théry, *Archives*, III (1928), p. 323.
[3] Printed in Preger, *Geschichte der deutschen Mystik*, I, pp. 483–484.

branded him as a heretic because of his teachings with regard to the Beatific Vision.

If the Franciscans took the initiative in the prosecution of Eckhart it must be added in all fairness that there seems to have been opposition in the Dominican Order itself. It remains to be proved that John XXII was influenced in his action by pressure from the Franciscans. He handed over the investigation to theologians of note and their decision was adopted.[1]

We cannot acquit the prosecution at Cologne of malice and wilful perversion of fact. Sentences were torn from their context, presented in a garbled state and thus a distorted impression was created.[2] It is noteworthy that the greater part of the propositions submitted at Cologne were absent from the papal bull. When viewed in a dispassionate light they were seen to be harmless.

Eckhart complained that one of the 'suspect' passages contained quotations from Seneca, Cicero and Origen. 'They can speak for themselves,' was his comment; he added that the remainder of the proposition was based on a text from the First Epistle of St. John.[3] Well might the good friar exclaim: 'Everything they do not understand they consider error, and what is more, they think every error is heresy.'[4]

In short, the proceedings of the Inquisition were not conducted in a manner that inspires confidence and Eckhart's protests seem well founded. But we cannot say the same thing about the Avignon process, which was impartially carried out. In accordance with the practice of the time, the condemnation only applied to the literal sense of the passages selected, not to the meaning that Eckhart may have intended. That these propositions, taken quite literally, are not in accordance with the official doctrine of the Church is beyond dispute. The only criticism that could be made is that the propositions were excerpts or translated passages, and not necessarily representative of Eckhart's writings taken as a whole.

It must be admitted that Eckhart had on occasion said things that were startling enough; taken from their context, they might seem pagan or even blasphemous, although the sense is always edifying if rightly understood. He was himself aware of the dangers that lurked in his writings. In the Prologue of the *Opus Tripartitum*[5] he warned his readers not to dwell on the apparent or literal sense of his words,

[1] Grabmann, *Neue Eckhartforschungen*, p. 81.
[2] See Karrer, *Meister Eckhart*, pp. 303–304, 313–315.   [3] Ibid., p. 191.
[4] Ibid., p. 206.   [5] Denifle, *Archiv*, p. 535. Bascour (1935), p. viii.

but to make every effort to apprehend his true meaning: 'It should be observed that some of the following investigations, propositions and expositions will appear at first sight monstrous, doubtful or false, but not if they are studied with understanding and care.'

He had a great love of paradox and was fond of using extreme or exaggerated phraseology in order to drive home his point. He had the imagination of the poet and the exuberance of the rhetorician. Is it strange that sometimes he is carried away by his own eloquence? How easy it was to give rein to his fancy when preaching to a devoted congregation who were filled with enthusiasm for his sermons. It was urged against him that the illiterate would take him too literally, that they would be unable to distinguish between what was rhetorically and what was literally meant. Eckhart does not seem to have been conscious of having deviated by one hair's breadth from the strict line of orthodoxy, but his critics were ever ready to pounce on an unguarded phrase or bold metaphor.

It has been suggested, and the suggestion is very plausible, that some of the Beghards charged with heresy at Cologne had quoted Eckhart in their own defence. This would explain Heinrich von Firneburg's attitude towards Eckhart. It is also noteworthy that in the attacks made on Eckhart by the Franciscans and in the text of the Bull of 1329, stress is laid on the fact that simple folk were led astray by his doctrines. 'Inasmuch as Friar Eckhart has led a large number of persons in the above-mentioned Province of Theutonia and in diverse other regions to believe and to publish abroad the same heresies,' say the four Franciscan firebrands to whom reference has already been made. It is interesting to note that Eckhart's adherents are said to exist in Germany and elsewhere in large numbers. This may be an overstatement, but it shows at least that his following was not negligible.

As an example of a bold statement that might easily be misunderstood, one might cite the last of the condemned propositions: 'God is neither good, nor better, nor the best. If anyone were to say that God is good, it would be as incorrect as to say that white is black.' Taken literally this is obviously heretical. At the same time anyone who has even a superficial acquaintance with scholastic philosophy, or who has a modicum of philosophical training, would see Eckhart's meaning, even without the context. All he is trying to do is to point out that we cannot apply finite predicates to God as to any finite creature. There is, of course, a sense in which we can say that God is good: it is of His essential nature to be good rather than evil. This is a different kind of assertion from saying that a man is good. A man may, as it happens, be good in some respects, or on some occasions, but his essential nature is not goodness.

In his defence Eckhart did not deny having used the words quoted. He simply said: 'Certainly God, Who is above every name by which we might name Him, is as high above them as white is above black. And it is useful to explain and to represent this to the people in order to bring nearer to them the sublimity of God so that "at His name every knee should bow, of things in heaven, and things in earth, and things under the earth." '

The main basis of Eckhart's doctrines was Scholasticism. He took over its dogmas, its phraseology, and its technique. He never opposed any of the essential teachings of Thomas Aquinas. But besides this stream of thought there is another which is in the main derived from Neo-Platonism. Plotinus, Pseudo-Dionysius Areopagitica and Augustine are his teachers. It is true that Thomas Aquinas himself frequently quotes these authorities, whom he held in high esteem, but in his later works he tends to emancipate himself more and more from their influence. Eckhart's predilection for the Neo-Platonic tradition is undoubtedly due to his strong mystical tendencies.

The dual origin of Eckhart's thought explains the paradox that this great mystic, whose speculations seek to penetrate as far as, or even beyond, the limits of the human intellect, this poet, whose intuitions flash upon the reader with the suddenness of inspiration, could also indulge in the subtle hair-splitting of the schools.[1] It is at first sight strange that a man such as Eckhart could spend so much of his time in the exercise of intellectual gymnastics. Were the mystic and the logician one and the same person? Had he a mystical and a scholastic period? This explanation is not possible because in his earliest writings we find both elements together, and we find them in every phase of his career, including the last. What satisfaction could he find in the arid disputations of the *studium generale*? They were not arid for him. He thought it supremely important to formulate the doctrines of the church, to find an intellectual expression for belief. The abstract terms of theology are for him pregnant with meaning, transfigured by living experience. In his ardent, vivid prose the dead bones are truly infused with life.

There are two main themes which Eckhart is never weary of discussing: God and the soul. The outer world, the sphere of nature,

[1] E.g., in the *Commentary on the Book of Wisdom*.

science and law, the political and social aspects of life, are only of interest to him in so far as they are linked up with the predominant trend of his thought. The starting-point of his system is that God is being, pure being, absolute being, the final ultimate reality. One of his favourite texts is 'I am, that I am': the name of God. If we wish to make a statement about Him, the first and most important thing that we can say is that He is, He exists. This is the orthodox scholastic teaching, but in Eckhart's philosophy the doctrine of being takes up a much larger place than in the systems of Thomas Aquinas or any other scholastic writer.

One of the charges brought against Eckhart in his own day was that he tended to obliterate the division between the being of God and that of man. On the other hand there are many passages in his genuine works in which he stresses the difference between the Creator and the creature in the traditional manner. As a scholastic philosopher, he laid great stress on the transcendence of God; as a mystic he firmly believed in the divine immanence, and indeed he needed no proof for the indwelling spirit whose existence he had himself so deeply and fully experienced. Combining the two doctrines, he develops the paradox that nothing is so dissimilar as God and the creatures, and at the same time nothing is so similar.

Eckhart distinguishes between the triune God and the Godhead. The former has three Persons, the latter is undifferentiated. This again is strictly orthodox. The Athanasian creed puts it quite simply: 'Neither confounding the Persons, nor dividing the substance.' In discussing the Godhead, Eckhart makes copious use of the phraseology of Pseudo-Dionysius Areopagitica, who says that God is nothing, that He is darkness, and so on, meaning that to define Him, to predicate anything to Him, is to limit Him, Who is infinite. Eckhart states this doctrine on occasion in rather an extreme form, but it is only fair to say that he did not hold that God can only be described by negatives. On occasion he uses analogy to indicate the nature of God, thus following Thomas Aquinas.

Perhaps the most famous and at the same time the most characteristic of Eckhart's doctrines was that of the *Seelenfünklein*, or spark of the soul. Neither the word nor the idea was invented by him; the word *scintilla* is used by Plotinus and Hugh of St. Victor; Thomas Aquinas speaks of the *scintilla animae*. But Eckhart was the first to treat the subject in the vernacular and to coin a German word for *scintilla animae*. The *Fünklein* is that part or faculty of the soul in which, or by means of which, the mystical union of the soul with

God takes place. It is the seat of conscience and also of the religious consciousness, and has thus both an ethical and metaphysical aspect. It is indestructible; even in hell it speaks as the voice of conscience. Eckhart denied that he had ever asserted that the *Seelenfünklein* was uncreated; and as he believed in the doctrine of divine grace, it is difficult to see why his views on this subject are so often regarded as pantheistic.

When describing the mystic union between God and the soul, Eckhart often speaks of the Trinitarian procession in the soul, or to use the language of Neo-Platonism, which he himself employed, the emanations of God. Incidentally, this is a very different thing from 'emanationalism.' Eckhart's Neo-Platonism is here purely verbal; one must not be misled, as some have been by the mere use of the term.

Believing as he did, that God is eternal, that His actions, unlike human activity, are not subject to the limitations of time, he argued that the divine activity by way of procession or creation is one and indivisible. The begetting of the Son by the Father and the procession of the Holy Spirit from the Father and Son, are eternally taking place. Since God is in the soul through grace, the generation of the Son also takes place in the soul. This constitutes the sublimest experience of the mystic. The materials from which this doctrine is composed are scholastic, but the emphasis and the peculiar form of the statement are Eckhart's alone.

Of the historic Christ, who was born in Bethlehem and suffered under Pontius Pilate, Eckhart has not very much to say in his sermons. He has much more to say about the birth of Christ in the soul. It is in us that Christ is born, suffers, is crucified, dead and buried, and it is in us that He rises from the dead. The manner of His birth is a mystery, but Eckhart regards it as the most vital fact in human existence.

We cannot separate the generation of the Son and the creation of the world as two separate acts in time. From the point of view of God, they are both eternal, and both one. From the human point of view they are two and the first precedes the second, but with God there is no before and after. Eckhart is fond of quoting the text: 'God hath spoken once; twice I have heard this.'[1] This leads us to a consideration of Eckhart's doctrine of time, which is derived, in the main, from St. Augustine and Thomas Aquinas.

Eckhart accepts the fact of creation in the sense in which this means simply the utter dependence of the creature on the creator

[1] Psalm 62, v. 12.

at every moment of its existence, and also in the sense that there is a beginning of the world in time sequence. A certain wiseacre (sciolus) once asked him what God was doing before the creation of the universe. Eckhart replied that there was no 'before.' Time began with the creation of the world; there was no time before the creation.

The problem then arises: is the world eternal? Eckhart replies, in effect: 'No, not in the sense in which God is eternal.' The censors at Cologne took exception to a passage from the *Genesis Commentary*: 'The beginning, in which God created heaven and earth, is the first, simple "now" of eternity; that very "now," I say, in which God has been from all eternity.' In his defence, Eckhart commented: 'This by no means implies that the world has existed from all eternity, as ignorant people think. For the creation, in the passive sense, is not eternal, nor is what is created itself.'[1]

It is true that these statements do not square with the first two condemned propositions, in which Eckhart was alleged to have said that the world had existed from all eternity. There are good reasons for thinking that these passages had been taken from their context by the Cologne censors and were hence misunderstood at Avignon. When Eckhart asserted, in the words of the papal bull, 'It may be conceded that the world existed from all eternity,' he was admitting the point for the sake of argument. He was discussing the point with the wiseacre already mentioned, who had asserted the eternity of the world, whereas Eckhart maintained the opposite.[2]

In common with other mystics, Eckhart was inclined to despise the world. If he mentions it, it is to disparage it. Or he may use its phenomena as symbols of some great truth. One of the charges brought against him was that he denied the real existence of things. 'All things are a mere nothing; I do not say that they are slight or that they are anything, but that they are a mere nothing.'[3] But it would be a mistake to regard him as an unworldly dreamer. He led an extremely active life, busy with administrative duties, with preaching and teaching and the cure of souls. At the same time he found the leisure to write voluminous works, of which some account should now be given.

His writings fall naturally into two classes, according to the language in which they are written. The Latin writings[4] contain Eckhart's philosophical and theological system, and were intended for the learned. They represent his work as a teacher and lecturer.

[1] Théry, *Archives, Edition critique*, etc., 1926, p. 194.   [2] Denifle, *Archiv*, II, p. 553.
[3] Article 26, Denifle, *Archiv*, II, p. 639.   [4] See Bibliography for the editions.

The vernacular works were written for the laymen and nuns and are hence in a more popular style.

The most important of the former is the *Opus Tripartitum*, written about 1314. Only a fraction of this vast work survives. As the title indicates, it consisted of three parts. Each of these had its own prologue and there was a general introduction to the whole work. The three sections were entitled: *Opus Propositionum*, *Opus Quaestionum* and *Opus Expositionum*. The second is lost; of the first the *Prologue* alone has been printed. We gather that the plan was based on that of the *Summa* of Thomas Aquinas. Considerable parts of the third section have been printed.

The first two sections dealt with systematic theology and philosophical problems. The third, the *Opus Expositionum*, was composed of sermons and biblical commentaries, two on *Genesis*, and one on each of the following: *Exodus*, the *Book of Wisdom*, and the *Gospel of St. John*. Two Latin sermons preached at the Provincial Chapter are expositions of passages from *Ecclesiasticus*. All these have been printed. Among Eckhart's earlier works are the *Quaestiones* written in Paris, fragments of his work on the *Sentences* of Petrus Lombardus, and a Latin sermon preached on St. Augustine's Day. Finally there are the documents relating to the process: Eckhart's defence at Cologne, his declaration in the Franciscan Church, his detailed reply to the accusations brought before him at Cologne and his defence at Avignon.[1]

The German works consisted largely of sermons; there are also a few treatises on devotional subjects. Few of the sermons were written down by the preacher himself. Most of them were either reported by members of the congregation or translated from Latin. The text is often very corrupt and should be used with caution. To base conclusions on these sermons as to Eckhart's opinions and doctrines without close consideration of their genuineness is hazardous in the extreme.

From the point of view of the history of literature, Eckhart's vernacular prose is of great importance. He is expounding to the people profound matters, and has to coin German words with which to express theological concepts. In particular, he has to create a new vocabulary of mysticism. The German language then consisted of a mass of dialects, spoken by people who were, for the most part, illiterate serfs. It was suitable for the purpose for which it was used, as a practical medium to express the ideas of the peasantry, their daily occupations and interests; but it lacked abstract words and was not

[1] Edited by Franz Pelster.

adapted for the use of a scholar. Eckhart therefore had to make new words. This he did either by adapting a Latin term, by creating a new German one, or by adding a new meaning to an already existing word.

He was a great master of prose. He wrote clearly and vigorously with due regard to the spirit of German, without pedantry. Such vernacular prose was scarcely to be found elsewhere in Europe at the beginning of the fourteenth century. His contribution to German prose may be assessed by tracing, as we shall now attempt to do, his legacy to subsequent writers, and also by considering the permanent gain to German vocabulary which resulted from his innovations.

Roma locuta, causa finita. The Supreme Pontiff had passed judgment and there was nothing more to be said about it. As long as Eckhart lived, he had staunch supporters in his own Order, such as Nicholas of Strasbourg, but the papal ban put an end to open support. After his death he had still warm, if secret advocates in his own pupils and penitents. Tauler mentions his name with deep respect and affection. Suso quotes him as 'a sublime master,' and in his biography we read that Eckhart appeared after his death in a vision to Suso, telling him that he was living in Paradise and in the presence of God.[1]

Whether this is to be taken literally or not is doubtful, but it is at least certain that Suso quoted his master very fully and fairly and defended him with great skill in one of his most important works.[2] Eckhart was well known and highly revered in two Swiss convents, Töss near Winterthur and Ötenbach near Zurich. At Töss the Dominican nun Elsbeth Stagel, the friend and confidante of Suso, asked for guidance about the teachings of Eckhart,[3] while at Ötenbach Elsbeth von Begenhofen recorded the fact that she had consulted Eckhart about her own personal difficulties.[4] Queen Agnes of Hungary enjoyed the friendship of Eckhart, who dedicated to her his *Buch der geistlichen Tröstung*, to console her in her bereavement. It is not clear whether the occasion was the murder of her father, King Albrecht I, in 1308, or the death of her mother, Queen Elisabeth, in 1313.

There are some charming little anecdotes written in Strasbourg and Cologne by friars and nuns who had known Eckhart personally or by repute, which show in what regard and veneration he was held.[5] It is evident that his contemporary fame owed much to the

[1] Des Dieners Leben, cap. vi (*Susos Werke*, herausg. Bihlmeyer, pp. 22–23).
[2] *Büchlein der Wahrheit*, cap. vi.   [3] Des Dieners Leben, cap. xxxiii.
[4] *Die Stiftung des Klosters Ötenbach*, p. 263.   [5] Pfeiffer, pp. 624–627.

power of the spoken word. The living presence of the teacher and preacher inspired his hearers, but when this generation had passed away his memory slowly faded. A century after his death he was remembered merely as a dangerous and suspect friar. In 1430 the Divinity Faculty of Heidelberg University solemnly condemned his 'errors.' They might have saved themselves the trouble: he was all but forgotten.

In the almost total eclipse that followed there was one short interlude. Johannes Wenck, Rector of the Divinity Faculty at Heidelberg, wrote a vigorous attack[1] on pantheists, heretics, Beghards and Lollards, among whom he reckoned Eckhart and Nicholas of Cues or Cusanus. Wenck charged Eckhart with several heresies, for example, with putting man and God on an equal footing. In support of his contention he quoted the passage 'The Father begets His Son in me and I am there the same Son and not another.' This is the first article from the sermons in the Cologne indictment, and it shows that Wenck drew his materials from the official documents of the process.

Nicholas of Cues replied in his *Apologia Doctae Ignorantiae*. In order to avoid direct controversy with his opponent, he made use of a device suggested by Plato's dialogues. He invented a disciple who writes to a fellow pupil, reporting how he went to his 'praeceptor' (i.e. Nicholas), to tell him about the accusation of Johannes Wenck. The 'praeceptor' defends himself, and since Eckhart had also been an object of attack, he includes him in his defence. He says that he has seen many of Eckhart's works, but that he never came across the statement that the creature was identical with the creator. He praises Eckhart's talents and zeal for learning, but there is a note of caution in his praise. He would like Eckhart's works to be removed from libraries; they are dangerous for the common people, since they go beyond accepted belief, 'but they contain subtle and useful things for the intelligent.'

Evidently Cusanus had a close acquaintance with the works of his great fellow Dominican. He discovered a copy of the *Opus Tripartitum* in the library of Cues. He had it copied and diligently annotated it with his own hand. This manuscript of Eckhart's Latin works is the completest and most accurate that has come down to us. It is interesting to note that Cusanus occasionally adds in the margin 'Cave' (beware) beside some of Eckhart's bold sayings. After this short-lived revival the Latin works of Eckhart fell into oblivion. They remained buried for four centuries in the libraries of Erfurt,

[1] *Ignota Litteratura.*

Cues and Trier. It is true that Trithemius saw them about the year 1493,[1] but he does not appear to have read them.

This does not mean that Eckhart's influence ceased. By many channels his thought proceeded down the ages and continued to bear fruit in other minds. The debt of Tauler and Suso to their master was immense. Marquard von Lindau owed much to him;[2] Jordanus of Quedlinburg plagiarized him copiously.[3] Less certain is the indebtedness of the great Flemish mystic Ruysbroeck and Thomas à Kempis. Some scholars have come to the conclusion that the former knew Eckhart's writings well and was profoundly influenced by them. But Ruysbroeck very rarely quotes other writers, and where his thought corresponds closely to that of Eckhart the indebtedness may be indirect, through Tauler, whom Ruysbroeck knew well. It must also be remembered that mysticism was 'in the air' at the time and similarity in expression is not enough to prove borrowing. In the *Imitation of Christ* we find many passages that remind us of Eckhart[4] but nothing that can be called an unmistakable case of literary influence.

The same explanation can be given for the similarities of ideas and general trend of thought shared by Eckhart and the English mystics, John Hilton and Julian of Norwich. Direct borrowing is very unlikely. Such influence as Eckhart had on Luther was largely indirect, through Tauler or Marquard von Lindau, for example. With regard to Angelus Silesius the position is quite different. His dependence on Eckhart has doubtless been exaggerated, but he knew some at least of Eckhart's sermons, and *Der cherubinische Wandersmann* (1657) has been aptly described as 'a seventeenth century edition of Eckhart.'[5]

The chief medium by which Eckhart's mysticism was transmitted to posterity was that of the German sermons and tractates.[6] Unlike the Latin works, these continued to be copied and quoted. Many of them were not written down by Eckhart himself, but were reported by others. Often they did not bear the author's name, or passed as the works of some other writer. Thus Eckhart's vernacular writings may be said to have led a kind of underground existence. The general fate of thirteenth- and fourteenth-century sermons was to be edited,

---

[1] *De Scriptoribus Ecclesiasticis, Basileae*, 1494, fol. 78.
[2] J. M. Clark, in *Modern Language Review*, xxxiv (1939), pp. 72–78.
[3] R. Klibansky, *Magistri Eckhardi Opera Latina*, p. xiii.
[4] Karrer (1923), pp. 253–254, 258, 261–262, 265–270.   [5] Ibid., p. 55.
[6] It was the German sermons that inspired Angelus Silesius, but he read them in the Latin translation of Surius.

cut up, excerpted and rearranged to form devotional manuals. There was a considerable demand for such literature in Germany. A new reading public had grown up in the towns and the demand was greater than the supply.

When the rediscovery of Eckhart came, it was the German sermons that first attracted attention. But before this could take place mountains of prejudice and ignorance had to be cleared away. In the Age of Enlightenment mysticism had fallen into disrepute. The word 'mystic' was synonymous with 'crazy dreamer.' Kant called mysticism 'Afterphilosophie,' which means as much as 'pseudo-philosophy' or 'sham philosophy.' There are a few notable exceptions to this general tendency. The Protestant theologian Gottfried Arnold in 1702 mentioned Eckhart as one of those 'pious and devout men who ought least of all to be compared with the Papists.'[1] But this was only a passing reference: Arnold knew very little about Eckhart. His knowledge was probably limited to what he had gleaned from the printed edition of Tauler's works.

In the early nineteenth century the reign of rationalism was drawing to a close. The die-hards still proclaimed the pre-eminence of reason, but a new conception of religion and a revival of religious consciousness were the order of the day. In some circles this revival assumed strange and eccentric forms. There was widespread interest in the phenomena of spiritualism, hypnotism, clairvoyance, somnambulism and 'magnetism.' Swedenborgianism and other strange new creeds became the fashion. Scholars began to study the problem of mysticism in order to combat it as irrational and unnatural.

There were two directions in which the newly aroused interest in mysticism found expression. First, there was an uncritical demand for reading matter, which led to new editions of Tauler and Suso and other mediaeval writers. Secondly, the rationalists and Lutherans wrote histories of mysticism in order to refute the claims of the mystics. The leading representatives of this school of thought were Docen (1806) and Heinrich Schmid (1824). For twenty years the attacks on the mystics continued, but meanwhile the opposition to rationalism gradually gained strength.

Among the pioneers was J. J. von Görres, the intellectual leader of the group of Heidelberg Romanticists. Görres was very strongly attracted to mysticism and found it congenial to his own cast of mind. Suso appealed to him in particular; of Eckhart he knew little. He described the latter as 'a wonderful, almost mythical Christian figure,

---

[1] *Historia et Descriptio Theologiæ et Mysticæ*, pp. 305–306.

half hidden in the mists of antiquity.'[1] As Eckhart's works were bound together with Tauler's, Görres thought that he was a pupil of Tauler's. The philosopher Friedrich von Baader discovered a manuscript of Eckhart in the Munich University Library, and it became clear to him that this was a mystic in his own right and no mere disciple of Tauler. 'Eckhart is justly called the Master,' he once observed, 'he surpasses all other mystics.' Baader called the attention of Hegel to Eckhart and proposed to edit his works.[2] He did not live to carry out the project, and it was left to Pfeiffer to be the editor of Eckhart.

Although Hegel's acquaintance with Eckhart was superficial, he regarded him as a predecessor and a kindred spirit.[3] It was naturally those passages that had a pantheistic tendency that pleased Hegel best, and he did not stop to inquire whether they were genuine or not. Schopenhauer was also an admirer of Eckhart, whom he quotes three times with evident approval.[4] 'It is probable that nowhere is the spirit of Christianity in this direction so completely and vigorously expressed as in the writings of the German mystics.' Schopenhauer conceived the identity of the worshipper and the God he worships, to be the very essence of religion and he found, or thought he found, this idea in Eckhart. It is curious to note that all the three quotations made by Schopenhauer are from treatises falsely attributed to Eckhart. The last, in which a nun is reported as saying to her confessor 'Sir, rejoice with me; I have become God,'[5] is from *Swester Katrei*, a composite work, of which one part (containing this passage) is apparently a tractate of the Beghards and entirely heretical. Eckhart himself never wrote anything of the kind.

It is astonishing to find that these philosophers, who claimed to be led by the light of reason alone and to be free from dogmatism, should be so uncritical. The theologians, both Catholic and Protestant, are more cautious. The very qualities that endeared Eckhart to the philosophers made him suspect to the divines. The orthodox Lutheran Franz Delitzsch (1842) denounced mediaeval theology and the 'Satanic abyss' of Hegelianism. He blamed Herder and others for identifying Christianity and mysticism. The philosophers had played off Eckhart against orthodox Protestant theology. This called for a considered reply from a real scholar. It came from Carl Wilhelm Adolf Schmidt, whose *Meister Eckhart* (1839) was

---

[1] *Seuse, herausg.*, Diepenbrock, p. 34. [2] *Sämmtliche Werke*, XIV, 315, 159.
[3] *Werke* (1925), XII, 257.
[4] *Sämmtliche Werke*, München, 1924, I, p. 450, p. 457; II, p. 701.
[5] *Meister Eckhart*, ed. Pfeiffer, p. 465.

intended as a counterblast to the insults of Hegelianism. Here begins the scholarly approach to the study of Eckhart.

Before Schmidt's work appeared Eckhart's name had often been mentioned,[1] but next to nothing had been known of his life. Now, for the first time since Cusanus real light was shed on the historical facts. It was doubtless his Catholic teacher Baader who first drew his attention to Eckhart. The actual amount of facts discovered was small, but it was at least a beginning. As regards the texts, Schmidt was the first to ascribe to Eckhart fifty-five sermons and four shorter pieces in the Tauler edition. He clarified the chronological position of Eckhart, Tauler and Suso. Where he went wrong was in assuming a close connection between Eckhart and the Beghards, in casting doubt on the sincerity of his recantation, in identifying mysticism and pantheism and in separating Eckhart from scholasticism, of which he was entirely ignorant.

Schmidt was a native of Strasbourg and he wrote with equal facility in French and German. In his French writings he signs himself as 'Charles Guillaume Adolphe.' Interest in Eckhart in France began with his *Essai sur les mystiques du quatorzième siècle* (1836), in which it is claimed that Eckhart was a native of Strasbourg. A pupil of Schmidt, Auguste Jundt (1871, 1875), elaborated the conclusions of Schmidt and added considerably to our knowledge by the publication of new texts. Jundt's attitude, put briefly, is that Eckhart was a monist; 'Dieu seul existe, et que le monde n'a pas de réalité en lui-même.' He was, in fact, a pantheist, and was connected with the heretical Beghards.

Delacroix follows the same line of tradition. He gives a very fully documented account and sums up his opinion by the words 'Le fonds de l'âme est la divinité lui-même.' He does not accept the dependence of Eckhart on Scholasticism and denies that he held the doctrine of divine grace: 'Tout ce qui s'accomplit dans l'âme s'y fait par nature et par nécessité.' Where Eckhart is orthodox, Delacroix thinks he is afraid of his own audacity and tempers his doctrine to make it agree with dogma. His recantation only applied to two tenets. One might point out that many of the quotations of Delacroix are from spurious works. Perhaps he oversimplifies the problem.

Dr. W. R. Inge[2] agrees with the main contentions of Delacroix and states the view that Eckhart's doctrines were identical with those of Plotinus. Other notable French scholars who contributed to our

---

[1] For further details see the excellent account in *Gottfried Fischer, Geschichte*, pp. 15–21, 39–41.
[2] *The Philosophy of Plotinus.*

subject are Vernet, Puyol and Lichtenberger (1910). The latter places the German mystics in the history of Christian dogma and assesses their value from the theological and the literary point of view. But we are anticipating: let us return to the middle of the nineteenth century.

One of the earliest attempts to give a systematic account of Eckhart's thought is that of the Danish theologian, H. L. Martensen (1842). He points out that the condemned propositions were taken from their context, but thinks that they correspond in the main to the ideas expressed in the sermons. He does not hesitate to call Eckhart a pantheist, but qualifies the statement by saying that pantheism is the very basis of mysticism and speculative theology. He places mysticism and scholasticism in opposition to each other.

He denies that Eckhart was a member of a heretical sect, asserts that he did not wish to leave the Church or to attack it, but merely to renovate it from within. He was free from the antinomian doctrines of the heretics. Even more than Spinoza he deserved to be called a 'God-intoxicated man.' He did not succeed in resolving the inherent contradiction of revelation and mysticism, the divine transcendence and immanence, and hence the lack of unity in his system.

Martensen, who had passed through the school of Hegel, was aware that he only knew a small part of Eckhart's works, but he considered that this did not matter, because his ideas were all of a piece. He consulted the sermons by Eckhart in the Basel editions of Tauler (1521, 1522), which was really a better source than those used by many later writers. The value of Martensen's conclusions is somewhat impaired by the fact that he is in effect just writing a treatise on mysticism and taking Eckhart as its best representative. He assumes that there is no essential difference between him, Tauler, Suso and the unknown author of the *Theologia Germanica*, and quotes from them indiscriminately in proof of his assertions. But in some respects he anticipates the conclusions of modern scholarship.

In 1857, after eighteen years of concentrated labour, Pfeiffer published his edition of Eckhart's German writings. He enthusiastically hails Eckhart as 'one of the profoundest thinkers of all time.'[1] It is customary nowadays to stress the shortcomings of Pfeiffer's edition, the faulty texts, the inclusion of spurious matter, the uncritical attitude to the sources, and so on. But in all fairness one must concede that Pfeiffer must be judged by the standard of his own day as to

---

[1] *Vorwort*, p. iii.

scholarship. A vast impetus to the interest in Eckhart and the study of his works was given by the new edition.

Pfeiffer was more concerned with his great discovery, with making Eckhart available to the public as soon as possible than with making an absolutely reliable text. It did not occur to him, and it could not have occurred to him, that he was unconsciously falsifying the picture of the master by printing the genuine, the doubtful, and the spurious cheek by jowl. It may be added that Pfeiffer, with all his faults, was more critical than many of his readers. He recognized that the last few sermons, especially Nos. 105–110, are not in their original form, that they had been altered or tampered with, both as regards language and construction. He freely admitted that the later tractates in the book are not so well authenticated as those which precede them. He hints that some of them are rather in Eckhart's manner than genuine productions of the master. How many authors on mysticism, and among them some of the most eminent, have perused the book and extracted its contents without taking the trouble to read the preface? How many have assumed, quite wrongly, that everything in the volume is authentic?

So great was the admiration aroused by Pfeiffer's edition that no attempt was made to scrutinize the text. Eckhart was hailed on all hands as the Father of German philosophy, as a mystic of the foremost rank, as a great master of German prose, the greatest the Middle Ages had produced, and so forth. The name of these writers is legion; they are often exuberant in their praise and uncritical in their admiration. Among the most ambitious and the ablest contributions to the subject is that of the Hegelian philosopher Lasson. He describes Eckhart as 'the central spirit of all mysticism,' since in him all the elements of mysticism are found in the highest perfection. With the help of quotations from Pfeiffer he strives to construct a system. He considers Eckhart's basic assumption to be 'the divinity of the soul.' He recognizes his debt to Thomas Aquinas, Albertus Magnus and Augustine, as well as to Avicenna, Plato and Aristotle,[1] and maintains that in his attacks on salvation by works, 'monkishness, Mariolatry,' etc., he was a forerunner of Protestantism. All this is highly controversial, but Lasson made some very valuable criticisms that have not lost their relevance to-day.

After the period of exuberant praise and uncritical admiration comes an age of ruthless destructive analysis. It was a strictly orthodox Catholic priest, and a Dominican friar to boot, who ushered in the

[1] Pp. 81–82, 86.

period of critical inquiry. Heinrich Seuse Denifle was a Tyrolean, a man of humble origin, who by dint of extraordinary ability combined with unusual industry had established himself as an eminent scholar. He had a first-class command of Latin, and being an Austrian, he was quite at home with both modern and mediaeval German. He joined the Dominican Order just at the time when the revival of Catholic theology, or Neo-scholasticism, had reached its culminating point, and was hence thoroughly grounded in Aristotle and Thomas Aquinas. Denifle therefore approached German mysticism as a form of scholasticism. It was his great merit to discover in 1880 a manuscript containing some of the Latin works of Eckhart.[1] Later he brought to light other manuscripts and also documents relating to the trial.

Denifle struck a controversial note from the first.[2] The main object of his attack was Preger, the Protestant historian of German mysticism, who had proclaimed Eckhart to be an original thinker of the first magnitude. Preger knew little or nothing of scholastic philosophy. It was not difficult for Denifle to expose Preger's gross ignorance of mediaeval thought and to show that much of the vaunted wisdom of Eckhart was the common property of scholastic thinkers. Many of his profoundest utterances were seen to be taken over almost verbally from Augustine, Albertus Magnus or Thomas Aquinas. The effect of Denifle's criticism was devastating.

In establishing Eckhart's relationship to his predecessors and in particular to the Scholastic philosophers, Denifle made a real and substantial contribution to learning. But in his desire to discredit Preger and destroy the legend of Eckhart the original thinker and father of German philosophy, Denifle undoubtedly went too far. He was manifestly unfair to Preger, whom he treats both as a fool and a knave. With all his faults Preger was a scholar. He had the knack of ferreting out hitherto unknown facts. He found and edited many of the original documents. In another respect, also, Denifle overshot the mark. Not content with proving Eckhart's indebtedness to others, he sought to show that he is not a clear thinker, that he is far inferior to Thomas Aquinas in depth and clarity.

The criticism proceeds on two lines: first we are told that Eckhart is muddle-headed. He does not know the difference between one concept and another, or he does not use his terms carefully enough. He confuses his terms, using a word in different senses in the same paragraph, without making it clear which sense is applicable each to individual case. He does not distinguish carefully enough between

[1] *Archiv*, II, p. 419.   [2] *Historisch-politische Blätter*, 1875.

truth and error, by anticipating wrong interpretations. Secondly Eckhart is, we are told, led astray by false doctrines inspired by Plotinus and Pseudo-Dionysius, adopting their terminology without realizing the dangers inherent in it. Preger made some show of defence, but it was an unequal struggle. Denifle smote him hip and thigh and damaged his reputation considerably. For some time Denifle held the field unopposed. No one dared to challenge the formidable Dominican on his own ground. The investigation of Eckhart came to a standstill.

After this epoch of destructive criticism when no reputation seemed safe, there came a reaction. It was seen that Denifle had overstated his case, that his views were not free from prejudice, that the manuscripts he had edited were occasionally corrupt and the conclusions he had drawn were sometimes unwarrranted. Scholars began to pluck up their courage and resume the formidable task of critical inquiry. The first steps were taken by Langenberg (1902) and Pummerer (1903). The former traced Eckhart's influence in the Low Countries, the latter surveyed the whole field of Eckhart scholarship and made some additions to it. More original documents were edited by Daniels, Bäumker and Théry. The publication of Eckhart's defence before his judges doubtless aroused sympathy for the friar. In fact, Eckhart came to be reinstated as a mystic, although as a philosopher he had suffered a certain loss of status.

Then from a new direction the critics made their voices heard. The object of their strictures was Pfeiffer's edition of the German sermons. Philologists began to raise doubts about the accuracy and dependability of Pfeiffer's text. Confidence in this work was completely undermined by the investigations of Spamer, Behaghel and Strauch, between 1908 and 1912. Spamer's investigations were carried out with characteristic German thoroughness. He consulted no less than 171 original manuscripts.

It was shown that in Pfeiffer's edition the same passage sometimes occurs twice on different pages; there are interpolations and corrupt passages; some of the sermons are careless translations of a Latin original, others are summaries of different sermons amalgamated and printed as one. Much of the work attributed to Eckhart could not be vouched for, and some of the treatises are not in his style at all. All the elaborate theories that had been built up on the basis of Pfeiffer's text now fell to the ground. It seemed as if the task of assessing Eckhart would have to begin all over again.

Some kind of order was finally restored in the chaos that ensued.

Positive criteria were brought forward for the identification of authentic works. It was shown that in the documents of the process the opening words, or *incipit*, of sixteen sermons were quoted, together with whole sentences from these and other sermons.[1] Here we have a reliable test to distinguish between the genuine and the doubtful. Many sermons bear the name of Eckhart either in one manuscript or in more than one. This is another guide. Further, there is internal evidence as regards style and vocabulary. In works that are recognized as authentic we come across certain peculiarities. Eckhart was very fond of rhetorical repetition for the sake of effect; and several turns of phrase recur continually. When these are entirely absent we may justly suspect the hand of another author. As a result of patient research a core or canon of genuine sermons and tractates has been established. It now remains to apply the results obtained to further material, always examining the manuscripts themselves to see if the work in question is ever attributed to Eckhart in an early and reliable text.

After the first World War, there was a certain vogue of mysticism in Germany. The pessimism that followed defeat and political disintegration fostered this tendency, which was loosely connected with the Expressionistic movement in literature. It was a reaction against materialism, an escape from depression, a release from the problems of the present.

The new fashion did not go very deep and left few traces behind it. Literature and philosophy were influenced by it to some extent, and it even affected scholarship for a time. Through the revival of interest in the great mystics of the East and West, Eckhart came into his own again. Much of the literature thus inspired was ephemeral, but there were some notable publications. There was, for example, a learned and earnest attempt on the part of Otto Karrer to reinstate Eckhart as a great thinker and moreover as a loyal son of the Church. Karrer was one of a long line of Catholic apologists of Eckhart, among whom we may reckon Baader, Joseph Bach and Linsenmann.[2] In the other camp we find men like Lasson, Hauck, Pahncke and Dittrich, who assert that Eckhart was at bottom a Platonist who tried ineffectually to make his real beliefs square with orthodox dogma. Even the psycho-analysts have delved in Eckhart. C. G. Jung quotes him on the subject of the Good,[3] and in his doctrine of the soul Jung seems to have studied Eckhart to some effect.

By the year 1930 it had become quite evident that the most impor-

---

[1] See Skutella for details.
[2] We may add one Protestant to the list, Heinrich von Ritter (1845).
[3] *Die Wirklichkeit de Seele*, Zurich, 1934, p. 210.

tant *desiderata* in Eckhart scholarship were, first a revision of Pfeiffer's version of the German works, or better still, a completely new edition, and secondly, the publication of all Eckhart's Latin writings. Until this was done it would be impossible to get a complete picture of the author's personality. The difficulties were formidable. The Latin manuscripts are written in a very abbreviated script, which can only be deciphered by the expert. It is not enough to be thoroughly versed in mediaeval Latin and its usual abbreviations, one must also be familiar with the special Dominican abbreviations of the early fourteenth century. A profound knowledge of Scholasticism is a *sine qua non*.

In 1932 the plan for a complete edition of the Latin works was submitted to the Heidelberg Academy by Dr. Raymond Klibansky, and he was entrusted with the execution of the project. In the following year the Santa Sabina Institute in Rome, the headquarters of Dominican historical scholarship, took over the direction of the work under the general editorship of Father Gabriel Théry and Dr. Klibansky. The individual volumes were to be produced by a group of distinguished scholars of British, Belgian, French, German and Italian nationality. The last volume was to contain a biography of Eckhart. Of the seventeen volumes that were envisaged only three appeared. The Nazi government sabotaged the scheme in every possible way, *inter alia* by refusing to allow rotographs to be sent from Germany to the editors and by threatening the German publisher in Leipzig with imprisonment.

An opposition venture, including both the Latin and the German works of Eckhart, was sponsored by the German government. The editors of the Latin works were Karl Christ and Joseph Koch; for the German ones Konrad Weiss and Josef Quint. Of the eight volumes that were planned, parts of three actually appeared. The outbreak of the war brought this enterprise also to a standstill.

Perhaps the strangest episode in Eckhart's posthumous fame was the attempt of the Nazis to annex him and exploit him. The remark in a sermon that the blood was the noblest thing in man[1] seemed to square with the National Socialist racial theories about blood and soil. They found additional arguments. Christianity is not, they said, a fixed and constant thing, but it exists in different forms, coloured by the nations that adopted it. It is, in fact, divided into a number of national churches or national religions, and its specific form is based on the racial qualities of the country in question. Eckhart was a representative of German Christianity or of German religion. If in

[1] Pfeiffer, No. 56, p. 179.

every individual the religious experience has a special, personal form why should not this be true of a nation? Are not Eckhart, Luther, and Fichte all representatives of German piety?[1]

Eckhart was coupled together with Luther as one of the heroic champions of the truth, men who would face martyrdom rather than renounce their faith. How are we to slur over the fact that Eckhart recanted? The Nazi argument is that his revolt was certainly not so obvious as Luther's, but it was an inner revolt. He is praised for his strong individuality and this is extolled as a German quality. 'No country has produced so many heretics as Germany,' proudly exclaims Walter Lehmann. Whereas Luther broke away from tradition with his eyes open, and did not shrink from the consequences of his action, excommunication, and so forth, Eckhart did not clearly realize the implications of his rebellion. He went on his way blindly, naïvely afraid at the results and the hostility of the Church.

Let us examine these arguments. The passage about the blood is torn from its context. The beginning of the sermon runs thus: ' "Fear not those who kill the body but cannot kill the soul," for spirit cannot kill spirit. Spirit gives life to spirit. Those who wish to kill you, they are flesh and blood, and they die together. The noblest thing in man is the blood, if it wills good. But the vilest thing that is in man is the blood, if it wills evil. If the blood conquers the flesh, then the man is humble, patient and chaste and has in him all virtue. But if the flesh conquers the blood, the man becomes proud, angry, and unchaste and has all vices in him.' It is quite obvious that Eckhart is not using *blood* in the Nazi sense at all.

The Nazis never realized how much Eckhart owed to Jewish and Arabic writers, for example to Moses Maimonides and Avicenna. When Goebbels publicly referred to him as the greatest of German philosophers he did not mention that the main trend of his thought corresponds to that of an Italian, Thomas Aquinas.

The conflict between Eckhart and the Inquisition is, as we see, interpreted as a battle between a specifically 'German' religion and the Roman Catholic Church. This is patently absurd. No one was more international in the best sense of the word than Eckhart. He studied in Paris, the intellectual capital of Europe, and carried off high honours there. He wrote most of his works in Latin, the international language of the day. The one thing that mattered to him was the religious life; he was indifferent to politics or race. The Order to which he was proud to belong knew no national boundaries.

[1] Walter Lehmann, *Meister Eckhart*, pp. 5–14.

CHAPTER III

JOHANN TAULER

THE ascertained facts about Tauler's life are not as numerous as one could wish, but there is no doubt about his birthplace. He was a native of Strasbourg and was born about 1300. There are various references to the Tauler family in Strasbourg charters between 1312 and 1349, from which it appears that they were prominent citizens and property owners in that city. It has been conjectured that Nikolaus Tauler, described as a citizen and magistrate, who witnessed a deed of gift to the Dominicans in 1319, was the father of Johann. This at least is certain, our friar was the son of a wealthy man; for he tells us himself that he could have lived on his patrimony if he had so desired. The family was evidently religious; Tauler joined the Order of Preachers and his sister became a nun in the Dominican convent of St. Nikolaus in undis, in Strasbourg. He was not forced into the cloisters against his will, but had a genuine sense of vocation. 'Once when I saw the holy brethren who keep the rules of the Order strictly, I would gladly have done likewise,' he wrote many years later to Margareta Ebner.

There is every reason to suppose that after the close of his novitiate Tauler followed the prescribed course of instruction, which normally lasted for eight years. If he entered the Strasbourg convent at the usual age he would be a novice about 1314, in which year Eckhart was prior. Whether Tauler was Eckhart's pupil in the technical sense or not, he was certainly his pupil in the wider sense of knowing the master through his writings and teachings, and he was profoundly influenced by them. He was evidently a youth of promise and was sent to the *studium generale* at Cologne to complete his studies.

Karl Schmidt maintained that he was also sent to Paris, and alleged in support of this statement, first the references in his sermons to the masters of Paris, and secondly an inscription in a book by Friar Johann von Dambach. Neither of these arguments is convincing. In the sermons contained in Vetter's edition the masters of Paris are mentioned three times.[1] In the first there is a comparison between a child of six and a master of Paris. Here the phrase simply means 'learned man.' In the other two passages the masters of Paris are

[1] Page 366, line 17; p. 421, l. 1; p. 432, l. 2.

mentioned together with those who follow the mystic way, very much to the advantage of the latter: 'The masters of Paris read big books and turn over the leaves: it is well, but these (the mystics) read the living book wherein everything lives.' This is scarcely the language of a former student speaking of his *alma mater*.

The inscription cited by Schmidt runs as follows: 'Friars Magister Johannes de Tambacho and Johannes Taulerii of the convent of Strasbourg in the Province of Germany, presented this book *De Sensibilibus Deliciis Paradisi* to the convent of Paris;'[1] the word 'presented' (contulerunt) does not necessarily imply that the book was handed over in person; it may have been sent by a messenger. It was natural that Johann von Tambach (or Dambach), who was a doctor of Paris, should give a copy of one of his own works to his old university, the convent of St. Jacques. It is not quite so clear why Tauler should have been associated with the gift, but one could think of many possible reasons. Only those Friars were sent to Paris who were intended for the doctorate, but Tauler's name is not to be found in the very accurate and complete list of doctors of the university. In short, there is no evidence that Tauler studied in Paris or that he ever visited that city.

In a list of eminent Dominicans in an old Basel manuscript,[2] Tauler is described as a 'lector'; presumably he lectured in his own convent of Strasbourg. For it was with his native town that he was most closely associated; there he found an active religious life and a great tradition of preaching in the vast cathedral. But it was there that Tauler had to undergo stern ordeals and trials, including voluntary exile for conscience' sake.

The Strasbourg Dominicans became involved in the struggle between the Emperor Ludwig and the Pope. In 1325 Lewis had been excommunicated by the Pope, and his lands were laid under an interdict. Four years later the ban was renewed and more rigorously enforced. In the imperial cities opinion was on the side of the Emperor, but the Dominican friars were loyal to the papacy. The inmates of the Strasbourg convent were allowed to continue preaching and saying mass for a time, but the anti-papal authorities finally insisted on the strict observance of the interdict, and hence the friars were forced into exile. They went to Basel, where they were allowed to celebrate mass and preach unmolested. This was in 1339. Tauler was already in Basel when his brethren arrived; it is not quite clear why he had preceded them, but it has been suggested that the Pro-

---

[1] *Quétif-Echard*, 1, p. 667.   [2] University Library, D IV 9, fo. 2.

vincial *studium* or school removed first and that Tauler, as one of the teachers, accompanied the pupils.

An entirely different version of the events that led up to Tauler's exile is given by the Strasbourg chronicler Speckle, who died in 1598.[1] He asserts that in 1341 a Dominican friar by name of Johannes Taulerus began to preach in Strasbourg and continued to do so for some twenty years. He vigorously condemned the interdict, as a result of which great numbers of poor ignorant people died unshriven. Together with a Carthusian prior named Ludolf of Saxony and Thomas, an Austin friar, he wrote many anti-papal works, in consequence of which all three were banished. Two articles extracted from their writings were condemned as heretical. The first dealt with the interdict and neglect of the dying on the part of the clergy, the second maintained the independence of the secular power from the spiritual.

Speckle's story is vague and contradictory, but he is so notoriously unreliable that no credence can be given to him. Writing as he did at the time of the Reformation, he was extremely prejudiced, and moreover he wrote two centuries after the events he professed to describe. The silence of other Strasbourg chroniclers and total absence of confirmation from any other source must be noticed. It is in the highest degree unlikely that Tauler, a Dominican friar, should oppose the papal instructions. For him obedience to the see of Rome was axiomatic. His friend Johann von Dambach had written a treatise on the legality of interdicts, urging submission to the Pope. On the other hand Tauler expressed himself on occasion very disrespectfully about secular rulers. Denifle has pointed out that it was permissible to give the last sacraments to the dying even at a time of interdict.

In 1343 the Dominicans returned to Strasbourg and Tauler followed them in 1347–8. It is not known why he stayed at Basel after the other friars had left. He paid a visit to Margareta Ebner at Maria Medingen late in 1347 or early in 1348. Shortly after his return to Strasbourg he became the confessor of Rulman Merswin, a wealthy local merchant who had retired from business to devote himself to religion. But apparently this relationship was not of long duration.

In some passages of Tauler's writings there is a kind of apocalyptic atmosphere. The sufferings of the age, the interdict and excommunication of the Emperor, the civil war, the Black Death, and the earth-

---

[1] The original manuscript was burnt in 1870. See *Suso*, edited Diepenbrock, pp. 35–39; Schmidt, *Tauler*, pp. 53–55.

quake at Basel in 1356, produced a feeling of impending doom. Well might people believe that the end of the world was at hand, Many sought refuge in vice, and conventual discipline suffered much. Both Tauler and Suso testify to the decline in morals. 'If I had known what I now know,' said the former, 'I should have lived on my inheritance and not on alms.'[1] There is a note of disillusionment here. The holy life that had attracted him as a boy no longer prevailed.

There is little information about the last decade of Tauler's life. According to Surius, the biographer of Ruysbroeck, he often went to Groenendal near Waterloo to see the great Flemish mystic, but there is no indication of the date of these journeys.[2] From the correspondence of Tauler's friends two facts emerge: the last Strasbourg period was one of great activity in preaching and at the same time one of great sorrow and distress for the preacher. 'They (Tauler and Heinrich von Nördlingen) have set the world ablaze with their fiery tongues,' wrote Christina Ebner in the Dominican nunnery of Engeltal near Nürnberg about 1350.

The call to repentance and stern condemnation of evil that resound in Tauler's sermons did not make for popularity with the general public. 'Pray for our dear father Tauler,' wrote Heinrich von Nördlingen to Margareta Ebner, 'he is generally in great distress because he teaches the truth as whole-heartedly as any teacher I know.' One suspects that Tauler was speaking from actual experience when he said: 'If anyone comes and warns them of the dreadful peril in which they live and how anxiously they should meet death, they mock him and say he is a Beghard and call us visionaries. They jeer and sneer at us as neither Jews nor pagans ever did to Christians.'[3]

We know that Tauler was in Cologne in his student days and again in 1339, but this second stay seems to have been short. Did he revisit Cologne between 1350 and 1360? Preger was at great pains to show that he did, and that he spent over a year there. It is true that Preger was anxious to make the facts fit in with his erroneous theories about Tauler's life, but we must take his views seriously. His argument is ingenious and intricate. Put briefly, it amounts to this: As the rubric indicates, one of Tauler's sermons was preached on St. Cordula's Day, which was October 23rd. At that time this saint was venerated only in Cologne. The gospel from which the text was taken is that of the twentieth Sunday after Trinity. The only year in

[1] Théry's interpretation of this passage (*Sermons de Tauler*, t. 1, p. 12) strikes me as unconvincing.
[2] A. Wautier d'Aygalliers suggests c. 1350. [3] *Predigten*, ed. Vetter, p. 138, lines 1–5.

Tauler's life in which this particular Sunday fell on October 23rd was 1357. Therefore Tauler was in Cologne in that year.

It is not possible to check all Preger's statements. One of the manuscripts he quotes was destroyed in 1870, and another, in the Munich library, may not have survived the last war. His argument rests on a series of assumptions, such as that the gospel pericopes of the fourteenth century were unchanged in the sixteenth, and that the table of festivals he used is absolutely reliable. But even if the date 1357 is wrong, one cannot help thinking that a residence in Cologne of a year or two certainly took place either before or after 1339. It may have been an extension of the years of theological study. It would follow his ordination, for which the earliest possible date is approximately 1325.

A considerable number of his sermons were found in Cologne, and an old local manuscript tells us that they were preached at St. Gertrud's convent there. There is also strong internal evidence.[1] In one of the sermons in question Tauler commends the Cologne custom of frequent communion, but complains that the sacraments are not always taken in the right spirit. In another he says that he has been in countries where the people are so manly and pious that God's word brings forth more fruit in one year than in ten in Cologne. This suggests a close knowledge of local conditions. A third sermon was preached on the dedication festival of the cathedral, as the opening sentence shows. In a fourth there is a detailed description of the building of a vast church. This could not refer to Strasbourg or Basel, where the cathedrals were completed, but would be quite appropriate to Cologne, where extensive building operations were in progress at the time. The sermon preached on St. Cordula's Day has already been mentioned.

Tauler died on June 16th, 1361, according to the inscription on his tombstone.[2] Quétif's date, 1379, is due to a wrong reading of the inscription. An old tradition affirms that he died after a ten weeks' illness in the garden of the convent of St. Nikolaus de undis, where his sister was a nun. He was buried in the cloisters of the Dominican friary. His tombstone is now in the new Protestant Church, which was built on the same site. These are the authenticated facts of Tauler's life, but a mass of legend has accumulated round them.

There is a Latin *Life of Tauler* that was often bound together with his sermons and was therefore regarded as genuine. It relates that in

[1] Vetter, p. 125, line 30; p. 130, l. 7; p. 377, l. 3.
[2] See the very full account in Corin, *La Tombe de Tauler*.

the year 1346 a Master of Theology preached in a certain city and people thronged to hear him from far and near. A pious layman heard of him, and after being summoned three times in a dream to do so, he set out to the city, which was thirty leagues away. Five times he heard the master preach and found that he was a kind, good-natured man and learned in the Scriptures, but 'without grace.' Accordingly he went to the master, told him that he had heard five sermons preached by him, and asked if he might make his confession. This the preacher allowed; the layman confessed his sins and received the sacrament.

After twelve weeks had passed, the layman asked the priest to preach a sermon showing how a man might attain the greatest heights that can be attained in this life. The master objected that the layman would not understand such lofty matters. The visitor pleaded, and finally the master acceded to his request. He announced to his congregation that in three days he would teach them how a man could attain the highest point of perfection and nearness to God. A large congregation assembled to hear him on the appointed day.

The sermon contained twenty-four articles or points which were essential for true holiness of life. After hearing the preacher, the layman went to his lodgings and wrote down the sermon word for word as it was preached. Then he went to the priest and read it aloud to him. The priest agreed that he could not have done it better himself. The layman told the priest that he did not practise what he preached, that he was a Pharisee. After some discussion he convinced the priest that this judgment was correct. The master said that, like the Samaritan woman at the well, he had been 'illuminated,' and that his faults had been revealed to him as never before. He promised to submit in everything to the layman as his spiritual adviser.

The layman told the story of his own conversion, how he gave up practising bodily austerities as an inspiration of the devil, and devoted himself entirely to God. He also related that he had converted a heathen in a far country by writing him a letter, which the heathen had answered in good German.

The priest asked to be instructed how to live according to the counsels of his friend, and to this end he was given an alphabet or manual, in the form of twenty-four sentences, each beginning with a different letter of the alphabet. The master spent six weeks in making himself perfect in these matters, even chastising himself repeatedly at the behest of his instructor as a punishment for his laxity. He then received further instruction. He was told to stop preaching and studying for a time, not to give his penitents any advice after they had confessed, but to spend his time in his cell reading his breviary, or in the choir singing or saying mass and contemplating the sufferings of Christ and his own misspent life, waiting humbly till he was regenerated.

When he attempted to put these counsels into practice the master suffered acutely, and in addition, his friends in the convent all despised him and thought him mad, his penitents deserted him and finally he fell ill. The layman comforted him and give him some delicacies to restore his strength. After two years of this life, in which he suffered much pain, grief and poverty, as a result of which he pawned many of his books, the master heard a voice assuring him of deliverance. He fell into a swoon and when he came to himself he felt a new strength and a clear understanding of things which had hitherto been obscure to him. He sent for the layman who explained that now he would receive from the Holy Spirit true doctrine and the power to expound the scriptures aright; that he must begin to preach again; that the people who had despised him would now love him, but he must keep himself humble or the devil would rob him of the gift of grace. The layman gave the master thirty florins to redeem his books which were in pawn.

Three days later the master preached once more and a great crowd of people came to hear him; but when he stood in the pulpit he could do nothing but weep, and although he prayed for help his tongue was tied and it was of no avail. He became a laughing-stock and his brethren of the convent forbade him to preach again because of the scandal to their order. The layman consoled him and said that these afflictions were a sign of divine grace. He finally obtained permission to preach again in the convent, which was a convent of nuns, and spoke of Christ the heavenly Bridegroom. At the beginning of the sermon he said that two years or more had passed since he preached to them and the sermon was then on the twenty-four articles necessary to perfect godliness.

After this the master said Mass and gave Communion to the people. Twelve persons who had been in the church fell into a trance in the churchyard and were as dead. The master attained great fame in the city and was highly respected by the citizens. After eight years he fell grievously ill and died in great torment. Before he died he exhorted the layman not to mention his name nor his own in the book he was going to write nor to allow anyone in the city to read it lest his identity be discovered. After his death he appeared to the layman and assured him that his painful death was inflicted on him as a purgatory and that he was taken by angels straight up to heaven, where for five days he suffered no pain, but was deprived of the beatific vision. He was then permitted to enjoy the bliss of paradise. The layman also came to a blessed end.

Quétif-Echard and other scholars have pointed out various suspicious circumstances about this story. In fact it will not stand critical examination. How does it come about that a layman had to travel thirty leagues, that is to say some 150 miles, to hear good sermons? Surely he would have found eloquent friars in his own town or in the nearest city. As we have seen, Tauler had never studied at Paris and was not entitled to the prefix 'Master' or 'Magister.' Is it likely that a man of his learning and distinction should have to accept the teaching of a layman, however pious he may have been?

Quite apart from these points, there are plenty of other reasons for being sceptical about this story. It belongs to a special type of devotional tale, in which the characters are usually a priest and a layman, the latter gets the better of the former and shows him the way to true religion. It is all part of what we might call propaganda; the anti-clerical bias betrays the layman-author. It will be remembered that such a story grew up round the figure of Eckhart.

Denifle proved that Tauler and the Master of the story could not be the same person. He did more, he showed how the legend had grown up, step by step. It was not until the sixteenth century that it was associated with the name of Tauler. In a series of masterly articles Denifle revealed Rulman Merswin as the author of the fictitious narrative. The 'layman' is an invention on the part of Merswin, just as the 'Master' is.

We have dealt with the spurious *Vita* or *Historie*, as it is also called, in some detail because of its importance. For centuries this inferior production has coloured the personality of Tauler as seen by scholars. Long after Denifle had exploded the myth in 1880, it reappeared and even in our own day it is not forgotten. An English translation of the *Vita* by Susannah Winkworth appeared in 1857, together with an English version of some of Tauler's sermons and a preface by Charles Kingsley. In 1887 the *Life of Tauler* was reprinted at Philadelphia. Even eminent scholars continue to treat it as gospel, because they have not made themselves sufficiently familiar with the literature of the subject.

After the *Life* had been proved spurious, all the treatises attributed to Tauler were similarly deprived of their claim to genuineness.

First *The Book of Spiritual Poverty*, also known as *Imitation of the Poor Life of Christ*, was eliminated.[1] Then *The Marrow of the Soul* (*Medulla Animae*), the *Divine Institutions*, the *Exercises on the Life and Passion of our Saviour Jesus Christ*,[2] and finally the *Prophecies of the Enlightened Dr. John Tauler*, were disposed of. As a result of this clearance of the literary field, Tauler has gained in stature rather than lost. He is more impressive than the banal 'Master' of the 'Life' and a truer representative of his Order and his age.

It was thought at one time that Tauler wrote in Latin, but this view is mistaken. All his works are in German. They consist of the sermons and one single letter to Margareta Ebner. The first printed volume, which appeared at Leipzig in 1488, was entitled 'Sermons, pointing out the nearest true way, translated into German for the salvation of many.' This was taken to mean that they were translated from Latin into German, but the original was in Low German, in the dialect of Cologne, and this was rendered into High German. The second edition[3] perpetuated the error: 'Sermons, turned from Latin into German.' Tauler had no occasion for using Latin. His sermons were mainly or exclusively preached to nuns and laymen, and he wrote no learned works, as far as we know.

As a preacher Tauler is usually easy to understand, homely and simple. There is occasional obscurity, but it is not quite clear to what extent this is due to the recorder of the sermons or the scribe who copied them. It is chiefly in the more mystical passages that the obscurities occur. He uses either short sentences or long periods of the Latin type. His language is often very picturesque and vivid, rising to real heights of eloquence when the subject demands it. He knows how to deal with questions of dogma or abstract thought by popular analogies and examples, and draws upon a rich store of observation and knowledge of ordinary life. He is well versed in proverbial lore and does not despise alliteration, antithesis and metaphor, though he is no rhetorician. He uses dialogue very effectively to expound a doctrine or to meet possible objections.[4] His imagery is derived from hunting, war, sea-faring, viniculture, farming, trade and natural history. But he makes a more restrained use of these devices than the Franciscans were wont to do.

He adapts himself much more to his congregation than Eckhart does. The latter is much more unconventional than Tauler; in fact it might almost be said that Eckhart's sermons are monologues, bold

---

[1] See *Das Buch von geistlicher Armut, herausg.*, Denifle; Ritschl, *Untersuchung*.
[2] Translated into English in 1904 by A. P. J. Cruikshank.
[3] Augsburg, 1508.   [4] E.g. Sermon 72, Vetter, pp. 391–394.

flights of imagination which too often leave his hearers stupefied and uncomprehending. He was a poet and a genius, and was not free from the limitations of such men. If the two mystics differ in the form of their work, they also differ with regard to the matter. Eckhart sees only the goal of the mystic way: the union of the soul with God, or as he puts it, the birth of the Divine Word in man. This is to him something so near and so real; it is the one all-important reality. Tauler stresses the way itself, the method by which the soul can be made ready for this great consummation. We are speaking, of course, of Tauler the mystic, but that is not the whole Tauler. He has two different moods, the practical and ascetic on one hand, the lyrical and mystical on the other. The former predominates.

He had been trained in the art of preaching. He could deliver a set piece on occasion, dividing the theme in the scholastic manner, but this is not his usual procedure. The majority of his sermons were addressed to nuns, so that a more homely approach was required. There is usually the threefold division into introduction (*exordium*), development (*tractatio*) and conclusion (*conclusio*). He often proceeds on the lines of the old-fashioned homily, taking the gospel of the day and expounding it phrase by phrase; or he selects a single text from the gospel pericope and works it out in detail. Sometimes he seems to have no fixed plan at all, but digresses freely, even losing the thread of his thought at times.

So loose is the construction that Strauch assumed that the texts we possess are only summaries. This is not a satisfactory explanation, nor can we accept the theory that the apparent formlessness of the text is entirely the fault of the scribe. The sudden changes in the trend of ideas, the interruptions and digressions belong to the very texture of the sermon, and we are compelled to the conclusion that Tauler was accustomed to improvise. These are the impromptu utterances of a busy man, with the typical illogical breaks and sudden transitions of popular speech. They were suitable for the time, place and audience.

The condemnation of Eckhart had put an end to speculation. Henceforth mysticism was confined to safer channels. It is not surprising that Tauler is practical in tendency. He eschews the metaphysical and fixes his attention on the needs of everyday life. There is in his writings more exegesis than imaginative treatment. To expound the scriptures in the traditional manner is a safe policy. As a general rule, Tauler avoids the semblance of heresy. When dangerous ground is to be trod, he defines his terms and keeps well within the limits of the strictest orthodoxy. Unlike his great master, he rarely speaks of the 'spark of the soul,' but often of the 'ground of the soul.' It means very much the same thing, but has no pantheistic implications. He is never weary of repeating Eckhart's injunction that God must be born in the soul, but he is careful to add that the soul is not God, that the Creator and creature are distinct, that they are of a different nature, that in this life we can only be united with God as a result of divine grace. Eckhart also held these views and said the same thing on occasion but he did not always qualify his remarks to the same extent. If Tauler omits to add the saving clause at times, it is generally understood or implied in the context.

Only once does Tauler mention Eckhart by name, and that is in the famous 64th Sermon,[1] which is so strongly mystical in tendency that some writers doubt its authenticity. Eckhart is mentioned third in the list of teachers: 'Of this inner nobility of the soul which lies hidden in the ground, many masters have spoken, both old and new, Bishop Albrecht,[2] Master Dietrich,[3] Master Eckhart. The one calls it a spark of the soul, the other a ground or peak (*tolde*), one calls it a beginning, and Bishop Albrecht calls it an image in which the Holy Trinity is formed and contained.'

There is another passage which is generally supposed to allude to Eckhart: 'Concerning this (the mystic union with God) a beloved master has written and spoken to you and you do not understand it. He spoke in terms of eternity, and you understood according to time. Dear children, if I have said too much of this, it is not too much for God, but you must forgive me; I will gladly make amends. A sublime master spoke of the perception that knows no way or form. Many people grasp this with their sensual minds and become sinful men, and therefore it is a hundred times better that one should come to it by ways and forms (by the usual method).'[4] Paraphrased this means: 'The master spoke of the mystic union of the human with the divine, but fanatical persons were led astray and understood this in a pantheistic sense, that is, they claimed that they had become divine and were incapable of sin.'

Many mystics are willing enough to speak of their own spiritual experiences but not so Tauler. He resembles Eckhart in his reticence, his impersonal treatment of religion, which accords well with the austerely intellectual attitude of the Dominicans, their dignity and lack of sentimentality. How little do we know of the inner life of these two men! It is true that there are occasional hints, but we must

---

[1] Vetter, pp. 346–353.   [2] Albertus Magnus.   [3] Dietrich von Freiberg.
[4] Vetter, p. 69.

beware of reading too much into what they say. Tauler's emphatic references to a change in spiritual outlook at the age of forty may well be due to his own experiences. He speaks of it no less than three times. It is, however, dangerous to jump at conclusions. In this way legends and fables arise. So little do we really know about Tauler as an individual that some writers have gone so far as to deny that he was a mystic at all! I cannot share this view: that he speaks of things he has himself seen, heard and felt cannot be doubted if we pay due attention to the note of strong conviction with which he always speaks of the union of the human and the divine; here is the unmistakable autobiographical touch.

Quite apart from his reticence, there is another barrier to the full understanding of the man. His writings are not free from contradictions and inconsistencies. In sermon after sermon we hear the friar preaching on orthodox scholastic lines, carefully avoiding pitfalls, warning his congregation of the dangers that beset those who seek after the ultimate reality. But we also come across passages, even sermons, which have quite a different trend. We seem to be hearing the voice of his beloved master Eckhart, the authentic and unmistakable note of the real mystic. How does it come about that the man who can express himself with such caution, such scrupulous care, can, on occasion, let himself go, and indulge in the boldest flights of fancy? One solution of the problem that has been suggested is that these passages are not genuine. If this is so, whole sermons are not Tauler's work at all.[1] But there is another explanation that has the advantage of reconciling the apparent contradiction.

One cannot help thinking that the master's tragic fate had opened the mind of his disciple to the dangers of discussing the profounder mysteries of theology in the presence of untrained minds. The persistent growth of error had revealed the consequences of stimulating or permitting emotional religion in the cloister or among pious laymen. Tauler had seen what havoc had been wrought in the minds of Beghards and Brethren of the Free Spirit by the ill-considered teachings of an intellectual giant. He was torn in two directions. On one hand he did not wish to transgress the law he was in duty bound to obey; on the other hand he longed to speak of the inner secrets of the soul, which were to him an overwhelming reality. He felt the urge to pour out as his great predecessor had done in the same place, probably in the same pulpit, the story of the darkness of the Godhead, of the divine emanations, of the birth of the Word in the

[1] E.g., Nos. 1 and 64; see Müller, *Scholastikerzitate*, p. 418.

soul. Those who had felt the impact of the vast personality of Eckhart in their formative student years could never forget what they had heard.

Does not this account for the different reactions of later writers to Tauler's teachings? Some laid the emphasis on the practical side of his writings, others stress the Neo-platonic trend and considered it to be his real message to the world. Thus Louis de Blois, Denifle and Gottfried Fischer are stout champions of his orthodoxy, while Johann Eck (1523) and Petrus Noviomagus (1543) took the opposite view.

Tauler did not suffer such vicissitudes of fortune as did Eckhart. His works were widely read in his lifetime, copied throughout the Middle Ages and then printed in the late fifteenth and early sixteenth century. He was never forgotten and his fame never suffered eclipse. But the conception which succeeding generations had of Tauler varied with the age. Much apocryphal matter collected round his name and the process of rediscovery had to be made. Legend had to be stripped away and the truth sought out.

At first sight it may seem strange that Tauler, who was undoubtedly inferior to Eckhart in learning and force of personality, should have been such a powerful and enduring force in later ages.[1] There are various reasons for this. The ban on Eckhart suppressed his writings to a considerable extent and forced his influence underground, so to speak. In any case his works are more difficult to understand than Tauler's, which are admirably suited for use as devotional manuals. Tauler's practical tendency helped his fame; and the story of his conversion, which usually accompanied the sermons, made a strong appeal to Protestant sentiments. Finally the recommendation of Luther gave the Dominican mystic additional prestige.

In the critical years 1515–1518 Luther read Tauler with enthusiasm and not without profit.[2] The simple eloquent style of the mediaeval writer helped Luther in his approach to the general public in his pamphlets and sermons. He also gained as a theologian: he was enabled to acquire a new sense of the sacramental in worship and a deeper insight into personal religion. Doubtless Luther read his own ideas into Tauler and misunderstood him. He selected what fitted in with his own beliefs and ignored or minimized the rest. This was not unnatural. The Reformation was a period of savage controversy and acrimonious dissension; impartiality was scarcely possible. Neither

[1] See Gottfried Fischer, *Geschichte der Entdeckung der deutschen Mystiker*, p. 5.
[2] References in Grisar, *Luther*; and Köstlin, *Luthers Theologie*.

side erred in the direction of sweet reasonableness or tolerance. Quite apart from this, we must bear in mind the fact that Luther regarded the *Imitation of the Poor Life of Christ* as genuine.

Luther believed he saw in Tauler a kindred spirit and saw in his doctrines support for his own. He claimed that Tauler stood for 'evangelical Christianity' without any admixture of 'popery.' Four aspects of Tauler's doctrines attracted him above all: the idea of complete resignation to the divine will; the attacks on outer works as useless in themselves; the descriptions of the sufferings of the devout soul, its sense of being forsaken by God; and finally the attitude to Scholasticism.

It is true that Tauler on occasion commands the renunciation of outer works, if they stand in the way of communion with God, but he is not in favour of mere passivity or quietism, as some readers have supposed. He holds that even the sinner can do good and thus prepare for the grace of sanctification, whereas Luther's view is that man is in a state of spiritual death, from which he cannot be released by his own efforts. The mystics, and Tauler among them, are more prone to stress the natural good in man than the natural evil or original sin. They are incurable optimists in their own characteristic moods, however gloomy they may be in phases of depression.

Luther identified his feeling of alienation from God with Tauler's description of spiritual loneliness, but there is an important difference. With Luther the sense of isolation was permanent; with the mystics the 'dark night of the soul' was a passing phase, an interval between moments of intense bliss and exaltation. Luther detested Scholasticism and aspired to liberate religion from the shackles of philosophy, that is to say, of the philosophy of Aristotle. Tauler had no antipathy to Scholasticism. He often quoted Thomas Aquinas and other Scholastics, and always as unquestionable authorities.[1] He does deviate from Thomist doctrines at times, but not on fundamental questions. It was not Tauler, but Pseudo-Tauler, who spoke disrespectfully about learning. As we have seen, Luther did not know of the existence of Pseudo-Tauler.

As a result of Luther's championship, both Churches became interested in Luther. They contended, as it were, for the possession of his writings; each side claimed him in turn as one of themselves. But there were strange cross-currents in the polemical stream. In 1523 Johann Eck published a work in three volumes denouncing Luther and including Tauler in his condemnation, declaring that he

---

[1] See Günther Müller, *Scholastikerzitate bei Tauler.*

could not be regarded as a representative of true orthodoxy. Eck did not know Tauler; he was led astray by the Dutch Jesuit Lessius, who is better known as the main object of Pascal's attacks on the casuists in his *Provenciales*. 'Pour sauver la foi catholique, Jean Eck avait sacrifié l'orthodoxie de Tauler,' writes Father Hugueny.[1]

The opposite procedure was adopted by another famous Jesuit, Peter Canisius (Petrus Noviomagus), who tried to save Tauler's orthodoxy by sacrificing the text of his writings. Canisius edited Tauler in drastic fashion, suppressing whole sermons, missing out compromising passages, such as those which might seem to restrict the authority of the Pope, or which were in any way liable to be interpreted in a heterodox manner. Phrases too reminiscent of Eckhart were toned down.

Another powerful apologist was the Carthusian monk Surius, who zealously strove to separate Tauler's name from that of Luther, whom he abhorred. With this end in view he translated Tauler into Latin. It would, however, be more correct to speak of a paraphrase, because Surius' aim was to produce a version in polished Latin prose, making omissions or additions as he thought fit. His work appeared at Cologne in 1543 and there were twelve subsequent editions (Cologne, Venice, Lyons and Paris). Surius' Tauler was twice translated into German for Protestants by Sudermann (1621) and for Catholics by Carolus a S. Anastasio (1660). There are also Dutch and Italian versions.

The Dutch translation of 1565 was intended for the use of Protestants, which involved alterations, and for this reason, it was put on the papal index in 1667, which explains the often repeated assertion that Tauler's works were forbidden by the Pope. Nevertheless in Catholic circles, in spite of the efforts of Canisius and Surius, prejudice and suspicion clung to Tauler's name. The effects of Eck's animadversions were slow to disappear and the belief that Tauler's doctrines promoted Quietism caused the Jesuits to put Tauler on the index in 1578. In 1595 the Capucins, for reasons connected with the movement in their own Order, followed suit, including the writings of Ruysbroeck, Suso and others in the ban. It was not until the seventeenth century that Tauler's name was completely cleared.

Apart from Surius and works derived from him, there were many other French, Italian and Spanish translations of the treatises that bore Tauler's name, but none of the sermons.

In the Quietist controversy in France both sides appealed to Tauler

[1] *Sermons de Tauler*, p. 51.

in support of their views. He was popular in Pietist circles in Germany, but from the beginning of the eighteenth century there was a decline in interest. No new editions appeared for a century and such references as we come across in historians are superficial. Herder knew Tauler and read some at least of his sermons but strangely enough without being impressed. He admired his 'nervous language,' but dismissed his mysticism in a few words. 'He who has read one sermon by him has read all.'[1]

In the early nineteenth century Tauler came into his own again. The Protestants revived the Pietist tradition in which the love of mysticism was still strong and the Catholics re-edited his works as devotional reading to counteract the effects of the Age of Enlightenment.

The Romanticists were naturally attracted by Tauler. One of the founders of the movement, Friedrich Schlegel, drew attention to the numerous mystics in Germany in the Middle Ages; he stated that they were connected with each other and formed a kind of school. 'I will only quote one out of their number,' he continues, 'who is very important for the history of the language. This is the preacher or philosopher Tauler, who long after the Reformation was admired and enjoyed by both Protestants and Catholics alike until oblivion fell to his lot.'[2] He then comments upon the fact that the Alsatians, after their political allegiance was transferred to France, still retained the German qualities of thorough historical and linguistic scholarship. He praises the contribution of the mystics to German prose. 'If we compare their language with that used in Luther's time, or even a century later for such purposes, we find it is just as superior as the melodious verse of the thirteenth century is superior to the rough doggerel (Knittelverse) of the sixteenth.' There is a good deal of truth in these remarks, though it is an error to call Tauler a philosopher in the strict sense of the term.

Schlegel rightly attributed the revival of Tauler to Alsatian scholarship. Jeremias Jacob Oberlin, who was Professor of Logic and Metaphysics at Strasbourg University, read Tauler and in 1786 he wrote an appreciation of him as a writer; this was one of the first attempts at literary criticism of the German mystics. It was another Alsatian, Carl Schmidt, who later inaugurated the learned research on Tauler's life.

Other Romanticists continued Schlegel's work in popularizing

---

[1] *Briefe das Studium der Theologie betreffend*, 41. Brief. Carlsruhe, 1829.
[2] *Sämmtliche Werke*, I. Band, 68–69, Wien, 1822.

Tauler. Brentano read his works between 1817 and 1824 with Katharina Emmerich, at the time when his energies were entirely devoted to religion. Görres, the historian of the movement, devoted several pages to the life of Tauler in his introduction to Suso's works. His observations are a mass of errors, but his enthusiasm is evident. The philosopher Franz von Baader was reading Tauler in 1810 and four years later he called for a new edition of his works. Hegel quoted him in his lectures.

Until 1836 the attitude to Tauler was uncritical. No distinction was made between genuine and spurious works; there was no attempt to investigate the facts of his life. The Romantic poets and philosophers quoted Tauler without troubling to find out either what he actually said or what he meant by it. At the same time mystical authors and especially Tauler were reprinted and came on the market as popular devotional reading. This work was almost entirely in Catholic hands. Reprints, not critical texts, were required.

In 1836 scholars began to turn their attention to the matter: Pischon edited three fragments by Tauler and called for a critical edition of the sermons. In the same year Carl Schmidt's first book on mysticism appeared and in 1841 his life of Tauler. These works led to the rediscovery of Tauler in the world of learning, which for a generation was almost a Protestant monopoly. Schmidt, Jundt and Preger discovered new facts and discarded errors, but their theories were often hasty and ill-considered. Their method was faulty; they are given to making sweeping assertions on scanty evidence, of trying to make facts fit their preconceived notions.

It was the merit of Schmidt to assemble everything that was known about Tauler and add many new details. He was the first to undertake to divide the work of Eckhart and Tauler in the Basel edition. He clarified the relation between these writers and their relationship with Suso, though not fully. For Schmidt thought he could detect in the two pupils the pantheism of the master. He showed that three of the treatises ascribed to Tauler were not genuine. His biography of Tauler offers a mass of material, but it is not sufficiently sifted. Schmidt accepted the story of Tauler's conversion by a layman with all that it involved, in spite of the well-founded objections of Echard and Pischon. He followed Görres in retelling Speckle's remarks about Tauler and the interdict, without suspecting their falsity. He regarded Tauler as a Protestant before his time, as Luther had done, stressing particularly the doctrines concerning outer works. These views long persisted among Protestants and have not yet died out.

Milman[1] called Tauler a 'harbinger' of the Reformation, and thought he was considerably influenced by the Waldensians, John Dobree Dalgairns, a convert to Catholicism and collaborator of Newman, wrote a book in 1858 which was far in advance of the research of the time, and was in the main a defence of the Catholic orthodoxy of Tauler.[2] He rejected Speckle's statements as a 'myth' and cast serious doubts on the identification of the 'layman' of the *Life* with Nikolaus of Basel. But he regarded Eckhart as a heretic. Dalgairns occupies an isolated place in the scholarship of mysticism. No one in Germany took any notice of him and very few in Britain.

A new phase opened in 1875, when Denifle appeared on the scene. Hitherto the Catholics had been very much on the defensive in the field of scholarship, as a result of the onslaught of the idealist philosophers. Now the Catholics pass over to the attack and the Protestants, more particularly Preger, beat a rearguard action. The end of this phase was that the story of Tauler's conversion was relegated to legend, and all the *Gottesfreund* literature exposed as fictitious. The idea of Tauler as a precursor of the Reformation was rudely shaken. Discerning and well-informed Protestant critics have very largely abandoned the claims of Preger. With commendable caution the Lutheran theologian Ferdinand Cohrs observes: 'Yet Tauler is fundamentally mediaeval and non-evangelical and the Reformation elements that are to be found in him do not really belong to his system.'[3] Catholic writers would go still further and reject the idea of Protestant ideas in Tauler root and branch.

From about 1880 onwards interest in Tauler has waned somewhat owing to the lack of new sources of information and to various other reasons. As he has receded, Eckhart has gained in popularity. The one important event that still needs recording is the publication of Vetter's standard edition in 1911. It is defective in many respects, being based on five manuscripts only out of eighty or so. Of these five manuscripts two, those of Engelberg and Freiburg, are no doubt excellent, but the three Strasbourg versions were never seen by Vetter, who had to depend on very unreliable transcripts made by Schmidt.[4] Two of these Strasbourg manuscripts were destroyed during the bombardment of Strasbourg in 1870, a fact which German writers pass over rather lightly, and French scholars duly stress. The third Strasbourg manuscript, which was believed to have been burnt in 1870, turned up in Berlin and was finally returned to Strasbourg.

---

[1] *History of Latin Christianity*, London, 1855, Vol. VI, p. 560.
[2] *The German Mystics of the Fourteenth Century.*   [3] p. 456.   [4] See Rieder, 1912.

Of the eighty-one sermons in Vetter's edition, two are doubtful.[1]
Two others are parts of the same sermon for Epiphany and seem to
have been transposed.[2] No. 9 is a formula for general confession;
Nos. 58 and 79 are short treatises not sermons. No. 79 is an excerpt
from Ruysbroeck's *Vanden vier bekoryngen*.[3] Vetter omitted from his
edition two sermons from the Strasbourg manuscript A89, which
were printed later by Helander. Other genuine pieces, either complete
or fragmentary, are to be found in German, Dutch or Swiss libraries,
in manuscript form or in early printed books. It will be a task for the
future to sift this material and prepare the way for a new edition. The
first step was taken by Strauch in 1920.[4] The difficulties are enormous:
much of Tauler's work was written down by his hearers and suffered
in the process. These texts then passed through the hands of various
scribes who added or took away as they thought fit, hence discrepancies arose. But when all reservations have been made, Vetter's
version is very useful and it has furthered the study of Tauler
immensely.

[1] Nos. 1 and 64. Some scholars attribute No. 1 to Eckhart.
[2] Nos. 3 and 4.   [3] *Lieftinck*, pp. 207–208.   [4] *Zu Taulers Predigten.*

CHAPTER IV

HEINRICH SUSO

WHETHER the environment of a man in early childhood is always of decisive importance for his later life, is open to question, but in the case of Suso it is certainly true. He was brought up in an atmosphere of chivalry, heard its language and assimilated its attitude to life. His native province of Swabia was the home of the Hohenstaufens and Habsburgs, those great families in whose hands the control of the Empire lay for centuries. Swabia was famous for its music and poetry; it was a great centre of the *Minnesang* and of *Frauendienst*, that chivalrous devotion to women that came to Germany from the troubadours of Provence and the *trouvères* of Northern France.

The greater part of Suso's life was lived on the banks of Lake Constance, with its usually calm, unruffled surface, in an idyllic setting of gentle acclivities, fields, orchards and vineyards. In the distant background stand the Alpine heights, serene and unchanging. Small wonder that the prose of Suso is full of the song of the birds and the scent of flowers, of sunshine and light. His style is often rhythmical and at times it bursts into verse and rhyme. A born poet, he loves to indulge in reminiscences of the mediaeval German epic and lyric.

In the Duchy of Swabia the traditions of chivalry lingered on longer than elsewhere, but in the late thirteenth century they were in full decline. In the age of the crusades the knights had had an ideal mission in society, but now they were impoverished and often degenerate. Many of them drifted into the towns and strove to repair their shattered fortunes by allying themselves to the new wealthy class of traders and craftsmen. Many a knight turned shop-keeper and served in town council or senate with acceptance. Thus it was that Heinrich's father, though a knight and a member of the Von Berg family,[1] with a hereditary seat in the district of Hegau, found his way to the city of Constance, and married the daughter of a wealthy patrician. About 1300[2] their son Heinrich was born in Constance, or, according to a less reliable tradition, in the neighbouring town of Überlingen.

---

[1] For further details see Kärcher, pp. 194–202.
[2] Bihlmeyer's date (p. 65) is based *inter alia* on the assumption that Eckhart died in 1327.

The father is described as a very worldly man, which suggests that his interests centred in hunting, hawking, tournaments, and jousts. The mother was a native of Überlingen, and her maiden name was Süs or Süse. The house of this family is still to be seen in the town. She was very different in character from her husband, being very religious and tender-hearted. Heinrich took after his mother; his frail health precluded him from knightly exercises and at an early age his thoughts turned to religion. To perpetuate the memory of his mother he assumed her name, probably after her death. This may explain the fact that later generations thought that the Seuse house in Überlingen was Heinrich's birthplace and associated him with this place rather than with Constance.

At the age of thirteen Suso entered the Dominican friary of Constance as a novice. Apparently a substantial donation from the Von Berg family secured the necessary permission for entry two years before the prescribed age was attained. In later years Suso's conscience was troubled by the circumstances of his admission. He believed himself to be guilty of the mortal sin of simony and destined to be damned eternally, until Eckhart comforted him and restored his peace of mind.

We are told in the biography that he conformed outwardly to conventual rules, but was restless and dissatisfied. He chafed against the strict discipline which 'held him to the chain,' but could not help himself until God, 'by a sudden change released him from the chain.' This is a poetic way of saying that he went through the experience of conversion, and what had previously been irksome became easy because it was invested with a new meaning and purpose. The change took place when he was eighteen years of age. Until then he had lived in much the same way as the other inmates of the friary, but their thoughtless, aimless manner of life and their frivolous conversation became distasteful to him. Their laxity was contrasted with his determined endeavour to fulfil both the spirit and the letter of the Rule. Consequently he underwent a ten years' period of strict seclusion, never leaving the precincts of the friary and practising the most severe bodily austerities.

These are described in the biography with a realism that harrows the feelings of most modern readers. He wore a hair shirt and an iron chain. His under-garment had leather straps and iron nails with sharp points. He had a girdle round his neck to which his hands were fastened so that he could not scratch his sores at night. He put on leather gloves studded with spikes. He fixed a wooden cross to his back with iron nails in it. An old disused wooden door served as his bed and he had no bed-clothes except in winter when he threw an old coat over himself. For a long time he ate only once a day; he abstained from wine and at times drank nothing all day, suffering tortures of hunger and thirst. Finally, when his health was so undermined that a continuance of these mortifications would have had fatal results, he was told in a vision to desist and he threw his instruments of torture into a river.

Suso was sent to Cologne to complete his studies at the *studium generale* of the Order. If we assume that the ten years' seclusion is to be taken literally and that it was not interrupted by a change of residence—two very big assumptions—he left Constance about 1328. This coincides with the time of Eckhart's trial and condemnation. There is no documentary proof that Suso studied under Eckhart, but the passage mentioned above shows that he knew the Master personally. It is abundantly clear that he was very familiar with Eckhart's teachings. He defended them with vigour and skill and had to suffer for so doing. He always referred to Eckhart as the 'saintly' or 'beloved' Master. His first work, *The Book of Truth*, is in part at least an exposition of Eckhart's doctrines in dialogue form. It is precisely those propositions that were the subject of the trial that are discussed and the exposition is such as Eckhart himself might have put forward. We are compelled to the conclusion that Suso's student years at Cologne fell within Eckhart's term of office as lector. For these reasons one would feel inclined to put his arrival at Cologne a few years earlier than 1328, at which time Eckhart probably had ceased to lecture and preach.

Suso did not go to Paris to take his doctorate. The reason is not quite clear. One suggestion is that he was suspect as the pupil and defender of Eckhart. There is another alternative, and one which finds support in the *Horologium*. Suso says that all the efforts of many scholars (at Cologne) were directed to their own advancement. They toiled in order to have leisure and ease. He himself was for a time infected by these vanities and began to aspire after worldly honours more than was fitting. One day after matins he prayed for guidance in his difficulties and was told in a vision that the best course for a man leading the spiritual life was to remain continually in his cell.

From Cologne Suso returned to Constance to teach in the friary school. After holding the office of lector for a number of years he was elected prior. The exact date is not known, but there are good reasons for thinking that it was in 1343–44.[1] At the general chapter of the Dominicans held at Bruges in 1336, the prior of Constance was deposed. No name is given, and it has been inferred that Suso was the person in question, and that he was punished in this way for his defence of Eckhart in *The Book of Truth*. Moreover, Suso speaks in the *Life* of a chapter in the Netherlands at which he was made the object of odious accusations, among them being that of writing heretical books. In the *Horologium* Suso mentions various trials that beset him and among them the fact that his 'chair of honour' was overturned and the 'grove he had planted' was given to another. These words have been linked up with the deposition of the prior of Constance, but there are chronological difficulties. The *Horologium* was probably written in 1334, and the punishment of the prior took place in 1336. From 1333 to 1341 Hugo de Vaucemain was General of the Dominican Order; he was well disposed to Suso, who dedicated to him the *Horologium*.

It therefore seems most probable that Suso was not the prior of Constance removed from office in 1336, that it was not the Bruges chapter at which he was tried, but some other chapter held in the Netherlands,[2] and that the punishment to which he refers in the *Horologium* was his deprivation of the office of lector between 1329 and 1333.

The struggle between Pope and Emperor had its repercussions in Constance. We are well informed about this period because a local chronicler, Heinrich von Diessenhofen, was an eye-witness of the main events. In 1339 the city council enforced the observance of the imperial edict which ordered that all services of the church should be resumed. Most of the Dominicans in Constance refused to obey and continued to observe the interdict. Accordingly all the friars except four, who chose submission to the secular power, were banished for ten years. Some found a refuge at Diessenhofen, others in the Scots monastery (Schottenkloster) which was just outside the city walls. Part of the community returned in 1346 and all were back in 1349, with the exception of Suso.

It was during this trying period of exile that he became prior. In spite of his unworldliness and evident ignorance of practical affairs, he seems to have ruled the exiled friars well and they were not disappointed in him. He even succeeded in paying off all the debts of the friary.

[1] Bihlmeyer, pp. 101–109.
[2] Bihlmeyer suggests the provincial chapter at Antwerp in 1327; see however Gröber, pp. 64–65.

The *Life* speaks of a decisive turning point in the Servant's spiritual development which took place when he was forty years old. He abandoned asceticism for good and entered the school of perfect *Gelassenheit*, which we may translate as 'resignation,' or 'joyful endurance and patience in the face of adversity.' With mortification and seclusion he also gave up teaching and writing. Henceforth his life was to be devoted to preaching and pastoral care. No longer confined to the narrow limits of his cell and his cloister, he now had the outside world as his parish.

There were three convents of Dominican nuns in Constance itself and eight in the vicinity. Doubtless this would be his chief field of activity for a time, but he visited numerous other houses.

He was an honoured guest at Töss, near Winterthur, where there was at this time a very active and vigorous religious life. Since Queen Agnes of Hungary had brought her step-daughter Elisabeth of Hungary to take the veil there, the daughters of many patrician and noble families thronged to enter its walls. While many benefactions assured the material prosperity of the convent, its religious life also developed, and it became one of the leading centres of mysticism in the Empire. Besides Dominican convents Suso also visited houses of Beguines. He travelled far afield, but his writings travelled even further, for during his lifetime there were many manuscripts of his *Horologium* in Paris and other places in Northern France.

The lonely ascetic had become an itinerant preacher, teaching, advising, hearing confessions, corresponding with his friends in religion. He became one of the acknowledged leaders of the movement known as the 'Friends of God.' Among his closest intimates was Heinrich von Nördlingen, whom we have already come across as the friend and correspondent of Tauler. Among his spiritual daughters the most gifted was Elsbeth Stagel, the daughter of a Zurich councillor. She was a nun at Töss and wrote the biography of thirty saintly sisters who lived there between 1250 and 1350. She also wrote down anecdotes about Suso's life, which formed the nucleus of his biography, as we shall see later.

The effects of Suso's pastoral work were striking. As a result of his counsels many women of high rank left the world to seek peace in the cloister. This often aroused the enmity of the male relations. The friar succeeded in the teeth of much opposition and hardships of all kinds. The physical toil of his travels was great: according to the custom of his Order he had to travel on foot in all weathers and on the roughest of roads. He constantly incurred the hostility of those who saw the stranger and failed to recognize the saint. The gravest of his ordeals arose from his ministrations to a woman of bad character who came to him for advice and guidance, feigning repentance, but abusing his confidence. Finding that she was deceiving him and had relapsed into her evil ways, the preacher refused to have any further dealings with her. Thereupon she accused him of being the father of her illegitimate child, and spread her slanders very effectively. Even well-tried friends turned against him.[1] 'My heart no longer cleaves to Suso as it did,' wrote Heinrich von Nördlingen to Margareta Ebner.

It is thought that Suso's departure from Constance to Ulm about 1348 was occasioned by this scandal, and we can probably identify Suso with the prior of Constance who was deposed in the same year. A chapter, apparently a provincial chapter held at Constance in 1354, dealt with the matter and found Suso innocent. The new Provincial General, Bartholomäus von Bolsenheim (1354–1362), was his friend and patron. But Suso did not return to Constance; he lived at Ulm till his death on January 25, 1366, and he was buried in the Dominican convent there. His last years would seem to have been peaceful; he is said to have enjoyed the friendship of Walther von Bibra (or Biberach), a Benedictine monk from the neighbouring monastery of Wiblingen. According to the local tradition, they used to meet on the banks of the River Iller, with permission of their superiors, for pious conversation.

Suso has been aptly called 'the last of the Minnesinger': he was the lyric poet among the mystics. But he did not pay his court to any earthly lady. It was the Queen of Heaven and above all Christ, whom he calls 'Eternal Wisdom,' who are the object of his worship and affection. He finds the most beautiful and expressive language to express the aspirations of his soul and to describe his own religious life in all its phases. His work has inner unity in spite of apparent lack of strict form: it depicts his search for God, under the allegory of his love for Eternal Wisdom.

First he seeks in darkness, ignorance and confusion of mind. He is not clear about the way to his goal, and wavers in his resolution, but as more light is vouchsafed to him, the quest becomes clearer. In the opening chapters of his first work, *The Little Book of Truth*, he is seen as groping after knowledge. He has not yet attained clarity, nor has he as a writer found his own style. Naturally enough he imitates others. He writes as a student and we can hear the language

[1] *Life*, cap. 38. Cf. Bihlmeyer, pp. 129–130.

of the schools in this theological treatise, which is a kind of short introduction to speculative mysticism. There are definitions, logical distinctions, quotations from leading authorities; but these methods are used with discretion: there is a remarkable freedom from pedantry.

In the first five chapters Suso speaks as one who has as yet had no experience of the mystical union with the divine. He has heard of it and read about it, but it is unexplored country to him. He knows the current theological phraseology, but it is like a lesson he has learnt by rote that conveys little or nothing to his mind. He deals with the fundamental problems of mysticism: God and His nature, the divine unity and trinity, the creation and incarnation, the redemption of man, the union with God here on earth and the beatific vision of God hereafter.

In the fifth chapter we are told of a great change that has taken place in him. The revelation of the divine has been his and he now realizes the inadequacy of words to express the ineffable. He has been in that state of ecstasy in which there is neither past, present, nor future, in which we can understand without rational processes or mental images. But few are called to these lofty heights, he tells us; the average man must hold to the general teaching of the church, for union with the divine is not to be achieved as a result of our own efforts.

'False freedom and its perils' is the subject of the sixth chapter. The friar sees in his mind's eye a stranger, 'skilled in words, but unpractised in works, and puffed up with pride and vanity.' They engage in conversation: 'Where do you come from?' 'From nowhere.' 'Tell me who you are.' 'I am nothing.' 'What do you want?' 'I want nothing.' 'That is strange, tell me your name.' 'I am the wild man without name (*das namelos wilde*).' In reply to the question where his wisdom leads to, he replies: 'To unbounded freedom,' which he explains as meaning 'abandoning oneself to one's unfettered impulses.' The friar objects that this is not the path to truth. Everything that is disorderly is evil and sinful. The wild man cites Eckhart in support of his opinions. Cautiously and with admirable skill the friar corrects the Beghard by giving further quotations from Eckhart and interpreting them in an orthodox fashion. In this way three of the condemned propositions are discussed.[1]

This chapter is of great interest because it contrasts the doctrines of the master with those of heretical Beghards and Brethren of the Free Spirit who quoted him and sheltered behind his great name.

[1] Nos. 11, 13 and 23–24.

One of Eckhart's works, the Commentary on the *Book of Wisdom*, is specifically mentioned by Suso. There is a passing reference to another false sect in this chapter, namely those who imitate the life of Christ in outward semblance only, who are harsh and overready to condemn others and have no Christian love in their hearts. This indicates a rigorist or 'Spiritual' class of friars, perhaps the *Fraticelli*, whose animosity to Eckhart is well known.

In the seventh and final chapter, Suso discusses the nature of true *Gelassenheit*, through which alone the highest spiritual state can be attained, and how those who have reached this state should behave in various circumstances. This condition involves patience, renunciation, even passiveness, but not quietism. One might say that the purpose of the whole work is to show how true *Gelassenheit* is to be obtained, and what results flow from it.

The Little Book of Truth is written as a dialogue between the disciple (for so Suso refers to himself) and Eternal Truth, or the Beghard (in the sixth chapter). This form had been used before by Mechthild von Magdeburg and other writers, but they just gave a sentence or two in dialogue, and wrote the rest of the poem or treatise in the third person. Suso was the first to make a systematic use of dialogue as a literary form in German, and after him it became very popular with the mystics and Friends of God. The idea was probably suggested by *The Consolations of Philosophy* by Boethius, with which Suso must have been familiar.[1]

Whereas in *The Little Book of Truth* the dialogue is purely formal, that is to say, the disciple asks questions without in any way revealing his personality, in his next work Suso develops this literary device considerably and makes it a vehicle for lyrical expression. The questions of the disciple or servant, as he now calls himself, show great psychological insight.

Suso had tried his prentice hand at writing and in his second book he found himself as an author and as a mystic. *The Little Book of Eternal Wisdom* is a masterpiece of devotional literature. It is a practical work, written chiefly for nuns in simple, straightforward language, apart from those soaring flights of fancy in which the true poet is revealed. There is no theological speculation: it is only in occasional word or phrase that we detect the voice of the mystic. As a prose work it is magnificent: Denifle calls it 'the finest fruit of German mysticism.' The theme is not new; it is taken from St. Bernard, but the style is Suso's own. His purpose is to develop the

[1] See also Wackernagel, *Geschichte der deutschen Literatur*, Basel, 1879, p. 429, note 43.

idea that man can only know God through the humanity of Christ, through the story of His Passion. 'Per Christum hominem ad Christum Deum.' The germ of the book is to be found in the third part, which consists of one hundred Meditations, each of one sentence only, describing one stage of Christ's sufferings and death on the Cross, and of the sufferings of the Virgin Mary. These Meditations are divided into sets of ten and five and hence can be allotted to the days of the week or the hours of the canonical office. Each section is followed by a prayer.

Round this original core Suso built up his book. Like its predecessor, it is in dialogue form. The Servant (of Eternal Wisdom) asks the question and Eternal Wisdom (Christ) replies. In a few chapters the answers are given by the Virgin Mary, and in one by a man who died unprepared. In this general framework Suso weaves a narrative of great poetic beauty. All the resources of his vivid imagination are employed in depicting the sufferings of Christ and His Mother, the pains of hell and the joys of heaven, the purifying quality of suffering as the surest way that leads to perfection. The second part of the book deals with the right way of preparing for death, the way to live righteously, the best manner of receiving the sacraments, and it ends in a paean of praise of God.[1]

Suso himself prepared a Latin version. He made no secret of his preference for the classical tongue. He held that works written in German soon lose their life like fading flowers, whereas Latin preserves them. The title of the new book was suggested by a vision in which the author saw it in the form of a celestial clock, adorned with beautiful roses and with cymbals to strike the hours. The twenty-four chapters symbolize the twenty-four hours of the day. The *Horologium Sapientiae* or *Clock of Wisdom* is, however, more than a translation. Some passages of the German original are freely rendered or paraphrased, with many omissions and additions. Suso included some paragraphs which would have been out of place in a book intended for the uninitiated or uninstructed, such as comments on abuses in the monastic life and on political events.

The conflict between Church and State is depicted in the form of a vision. A holy man sees a ram with two horns wearing an iron crown (the Emperor Ludwig), fighting against the lord of the city (Frederick of Austria). Seventy foxes follow the ram. Most of the

---

[1] For Suso's influence on later devotional practices, e.g., the Stations of the Cross, see Bühlmann, pp. 68 and 227; Vetter, *Ein Mystikerpaar*, p. 115.

inhabitants of the city go over to the side of the ram, who has intimidated them, but a faithful remnant support their lawful prince. The leader of the sons of God (Pope John XXII) comes to the rescue of the faithful. The ram now vents its fury against the Pontiff and tries to thrust him from his throne, but in vain. The ram wins over the prince by cunning, and obtains the supreme power, but the sons of God pray for deliverance and their prayer is answered by the sudden discomfiture of the ram.

Apart from the question of the literary value of Latin, Suso had another motive for translating his *Book of Eternal Wisdom*. He wished to submit his work to the General of the Order of Preachers for his inspection and approval. The General, Hugo de Vaucemain, was a Frenchman and could not be expected to read it in the original. As Suso's first work had aroused suspicion it was natural that he should wish to have official sanction for the second.

The maturest of Suso's works, the one in which we see his tolerance, wisdom and human sympathy to the best effect, is the *Book of Letters* (Briefbuch). In the original redaction there were twenty-seven letters, written to Elsbeth Stagel and other nuns at Töss. There is also a shorter redaction of eleven, a selection from the larger collection. Neither of these is what we should now understand by a published correspondence. They are not letters at all in the modern sense, but pastoral epistles. It is significant that the shorter series is called not 'letters,' but 'teaching'; it is in fact a manual of devotion.

In the original selection we have also a book on the religious life, revealing the confessor of wide experience and insight into character. He knows instinctively what treatment each situation demands, whether it be encouragement or censure, praise or blame. But we look in vain for references to current events, for little personal details. Any such allusions must have been eliminated before the letters were given to the public.

Usually we have the simple, strictly practical advice of the father confessor to his penitent, but on occasion Suso indulges in flights of fancy, lyrical effusions in his best style, of course only as a means to an end, never as an end in itself. He speaks of green meadows, of the flowers, the song of birds and contrasts the glory of summer with the cold, dead appearance of nature in winter. This is an allegory of living and dead spirituality. Here and there we even come across a phrase of the mystic's special vocabulary, such as 'the formless nature of the divine abyss.'

In the shorter collection the letters are abridged, sometimes two or more are amalgamated, omissions are made and the letters are grouped together according to the subject matter to form a logical whole. They form a comment on the religious life, beginning with the first phase; a nun taking her final vows and abjuring the world; passing through temptations and relapses from the first idealism, through trials of all kinds, including severe illness, culminating in the highest spiritual experiences.

One of the pastoral duties of a Dominican friar was that of preaching, and Suso did not neglect this duty. In the course of his travels through South Germany, Switzerland, Alsace, and down the Rhine from Basel through Strasbourg to Aix-la-Chapelle, perhaps even into the Low Countries, he must have preached often. But evidently this was not his *forte*, because otherwise we could not explain the fact that only four sermons are attributed to him in the printed editions. The first is described in the *Life* as 'one of his (the Servant's) sermons.'[1] The fourth also is genuine;[2] the other two are doubtful. Probably there are other sermons by Suso scattered in mediaeval manuscripts. The matter deserves further investigation. As a preacher Suso does not rank as high as Eckhart or Tauler, and his sermons are not equal in literary value to his other works. They are simple, unsophisticated addresses to nuns or Beguines. But if Suso was no orator in the pulpit, he was popular, and tradition preserved his name as a preacher to the people.[3]

There remain two other works included in some editions: the *Minnebüchlein*, or *Little Book of Love*, and *The Book of the Nine Rocks* (Neunfelsenbuch). The former was discovered at Zurich by Preger, who proclaimed that it was by Suso, although there is no indication of authorship in the original manuscript. There are certainly many similarities between this work and the writings of Suso, as regards vocabulary, style and trend of thought. There are references to his betrothal to Eternal Wisdom and to the letters IHS engraved on his heart. But there are also important points of divergence. There are Latin rubrics which suggest that it is a translation from that language, and one feels inclined to accept the view of Denifle that it was written in Latin by a pupil of Suso who knew his master's works and wrote in his spirit. The influence of Tauler and other mystics is recognizable.

The last of Suso's works to be completed was *The Life of the Servant*. It is one of the world's greatest biographies and has been frequently quoted by writers on mysticism. Whether considered from the

---

[1] Chapter 39.   [2] Bihlmeyer, p. 121.
[3] *Heinrich Susos Leben und Schriften*, herausgegeben Diepenbrock, pp. 17–18.

literary or the theological point of view, it is a classic. We see the author in all his moods, exultant joy, calm faith, harmony, spiritual uplift, and at other times, doubts, suffering or despair. He reveals his inmost thoughts with a clarity, simplicity, sincerity and *naïveté* that are truly astounding. He is a first-rate story-teller; the little anecdotes that are interwoven in the narrative are of great power and dramatic effect. The whole is infused by a deep love of God and yearning for union with Him.

The *Prologue* states that the Servant (Suso) heard of a saintly and enlightened woman (Elsbeth Stagel), who had suffered much tribulation and sorrow in the world. She asked him to console her by telling her something of his own trials and difficulties. He wrote to her for some time, relating such matters as might be helpful to his friend. When they met (at Töss), he imparted to her in confidence many stories from his own life. She wrote them down without his knowledge and concealed what she had written from the other nuns. He became aware of this 'spiritual theft' and remonstrated with her about it, demanding that she should hand over everything to him. She obeyed, and he burnt some of the writings she had given him and was about to destroy the rest when he was prevented from so doing by divine intervention. Thus the greater part of what she had committed to writing survived and the Servant added to it 'some words of good counsel.'

This means that *The Life* consists of Elsbeth's record of conversations with Suso and extracts from his correspondence, amplified by some edifying matter from his own pen. The first part of the book, consisting of thirty-two chapters, is largely the biography of the Servant and is complete in itself. The second part is not so homogeneous as the first. It begins with a short reference to Elsbeth Stagel and later mentions her final illness and death. There are some chapters that are episodes from the life of the Servant, quite in the same style as in the first part, but other sections are purely didactic and devoid of action. The last few chapters, though by no means without interest, are entirely of this character. They are doubtless the 'words of good counsel' of the *Prologue*.

The first thirty-two chapters deal with Suso's life at Constance among worldly and superficial brethren who had no understanding of his aspirations and his intense spirituality, and in whom he could not confide his visions and ecstasies. Driven back on himself, he bends all his efforts towards the quest for inner perfection. In order to subdue his sensual nature he practises the severest mortification and for years he never leaves the cloisters. Then follows the pastoral period with long journeys afield. We are led through all the phases of his religious life, through physical and mental suffering of the acutest kind, through slander, calumny and hate to final peace of mind.

Without regard for strict chronology, the main events of the Servant's life are grouped together according to subjects. Thus, the opening chapters bring out the central theme. We are told of the friar's first mystical experience, of his spiritual marriage with Eternal Wisdom. In the fourth chapter we read how he engraves the sacred letters IHS on his heart as a symbol of his love of Christ. The figure of the Servant, as presented to us in the *Life*, is that of a saint in his pursuit of the sublimest of human experiences. But he is no self-centred ascetic: for him the ultimate aim of meditation is action. He has the warmest and kindliest feelings towards his fellow-men and is ever ready to help others when the opportunity occurs. When his sister leaves her convent and falls into sin, he does not abandon her to her fate. He seeks her out and with the greatest charity and sympathy wins her again for the religious life. He is silent under calumny and false accusations, always returning good for evil.

The picture painted is sentimental, perhaps even feminine, but we must make some allowance for Elsbeth's modification of what she had heard and read. We must also consider that when addressing a woman, Suso, poet as he was, would incline to such language as would be most intelligible to his spiritual friend. But there are phrases which can by no means be described as feminine or sentimental, phrases in which the warrior ancestry of Suso finds expression. Is not his favourite expletive *Wafen*? It is a martial term, meaning originally 'To Arms'! In the course of time it came to mean little more than 'Heavens'! but it remained an aristocratic word, smacking of the castle, not of the village. Again and again we find the Servant regarding himself as a soldier of Christ, battling against the devil and his legions. In a vision described in the twentieth chapter he is clad in armour as a Christian knight by a heavenly squire.

We could not have a better example of Suso's mystical style than the account of his first ecstasy in the second chapter. As usual, the story is told in the third person. 'At the beginning of his life in religion, it once happened on St. Agnes' Day, after the midday meal in the refectory, that he went to the choir. He was alone there and stood in the lower row of stalls on the right hand side of the choir. At this time he was very depressed by a great sorrow that weighed down upon him. As he stood there, disconsolate and solitary, he went into an ecstasy and saw and heard what is ineffable: it was without form or shape and yet bore within itself all forms and shapes of joyous delight. His heart was hungry and yet satisfied, his mind joyous and happy, his wishes were calmed and his desires had died out. He did nothing but gaze into the brilliant light in which he had forgotten himself and all things. He did not know whether it was day or night. It was a sweetness flowing out of eternal life, with present, unchanging, peaceful feeling. He said then 'If this is not heaven, I do not know what heaven is, for all suffering that can ever be put into words, could not enable anyone to earn such a reward and ever possess it.' This blissful ecstasy lasted probably an hour, perhaps only half an hour; whether his soul remained in his body, or was separated from his body, he did not know. When he came to himself he felt just like a man who has come from another world. His body felt such pain that he thought no one could possibly suffer such pain in so short a time save in death. He then came to himself in some way or other and sighed from the depths of his soul and his body fell to the ground as in a fainting fit. He cried out in his heart: "Alas, God, where was I, where am I now?" and said "Beloved, this hour can never die in my heart." '

Nowhere is the author's literary skill seen to better advantage than in the little anecdotes that are scattered through the *Life*. There is the well-known story of the woman with an illegitimate child, to which reference has already been made.[1] There is also the story of the accusation of poisoning the wells that was brought against the friar and the tale of his meeting with a fierce-looking ruffian in a forest.[2] The latter insisted on making his confession and told the Servant that he had murdered a priest at that very spot and thrown his body in the Rhine!

Suso's writings were often used and quoted by authors of ascetic treatises and sermon-writers of the fourteenth and fifteenth centuries. We find his influence in Rulman Merswin and in the mystical tractate known as *Der Schürebrand*. In another mystical work entitled by its editor, Greith, *Lehrsystem der deutschen Mystik*, large sections of the *Life* and of *The Book of Eternal Wisdom* are taken over without any acknowledgment. There are slight traces of influence in Otto of Passau and the Decalogue Commentary of Marquart von Lindau, the leading Franciscan mystic. The Dominican Nider knows Suso and occasionally borrows from him.

[1] Chapter 38. [2] Chapter 26.

Interest in Suso was so active in the fifteenth century that one literary historian actually speaks of a Suso-Renaissance. It was chiefly associated with a reform of the Dominican convents known as the Observance. The nunneries that adopted the new order copied Suso's works and studied him eagerly. From these houses the movement spread to others not affected by the Observance, to convents of other orders and to the secular clergy. At St. Katherine's Dominican nunnery in Nürnberg, after the introduction of the Observance in 1428, Suso was the object of close study. In 1445 Peter of Breslau, one of the Reformers of the Order, preached to Dominican nuns in St. Nikolaus de undis at Strasbourg, and commended to them the 'venerable, devout father and master of the *Horologium Sapientiae*.' We find the same interest among the Clarisses, or Franciscan nuns, of Villingen, and their abbess Ursula Haiden, who died in 1498; and also in the Netherlands, where Suso's works were diligently copied and read. The chief representatives here are Johann von Schönhofen and the famous mystic Gerhard Groot.

The most popular of Suso's works was *The Book of Eternal Wisdom*. It had an immense diffusion in the late Middle Ages. Not even *The Imitation of Christ* was so often copied or so widely read. The Latin version, the *Horologium Sapientiae*, was equally popular. If we include translations, adaptations and selections, some five hundred manuscripts are known. They are to be found at Cambridge, Oxford, Charleville, Paris, St. Omer, Rheims, Brussels, Utrecht, Milan and in most of the principal libraries of Austria, Germany and Switzerland. There are Dutch, French, Low German and Danish translations of the *Horologium*. The English version was entitled *Tretys of the sevene poyntes of trewe love and everlastynge wisdam*.[1] It formed part of the repertory of the English parish priest;[2] there are many manuscripts of this work dating from the fourteenth and fifteenth century. The first printed editions of the Latin *Horologium* appeared in 1480 at Cologne and about the same time in Paris. The Cologne book was frequently reprinted and in 1492 an Italian edition came out at Venice. This is, however, a very bad text.

Complete editions of Suso's works were printed at Augsburg in 1482 and 1521. At the request of the French mystic Blosius, Surius made a free Latin translation of this version, which appeared at Cologne in 1555, and was reprinted in 1588 and 1615. Hence in Catholic circles Suso continued to be read, but he did not appeal very

---

[1] G. R. Owst, *Preaching in Mediaeval England*, p. 286, n. 2.
[2] See the account in Wiltrud Wichgraf, *Susos Horologium Sapientiae in England*.

much to the Protestants. His asceticism repelled them, his 'Mariolatry' did not please them, and they found no ammunition in his works for their polemics against Catholicism.

Surius' Latin version was translated into French, Spanish and Italian; in 1661 the Franciscan Arnold Hoffmann rendered it into German. In 1622 Daniel Sudermann, whose interest in mysticism is well-known, published Suso's letters in the original. The Pietists did not know Suso.[1] He shared the general decline of interest in the Middle Ages in the eighteenth century. The first writer who read him with appreciation after the Age of Enlightenment had passed, was Herder, who wrote a poem entitled *Eternal Wisdom* (Die ewige Weisheit),[2] which is a kind of poetic summary of Suso's life, as delineated in *The Book of Eternal Wisdom*; it shows intuitive sympathy with his trend of thought.

German philosophers were not particularly attracted by Suso. They did not find in him a cohesive philosophical system, as they did in Eckhart, and he was not intellectual enough to command their respect. Attention was drawn to him, however, in religious circles, especially by Johann Michael Sailer, later Bishop of Regensburg, whose name is associated with a Catholic revival in Germany. As a result of Sailer's enthusiasm Melchior Diepenbrock re-edited Suso's works in a modernized form in 1829. Görres, the famous Romanticist, wrote a preface which is not free from gross historical errors, but it shows that Suso had found an interpreter who was in some sense a kindred spirit.

In 1843 Carl Schmidt attempted a complete survey of Suso's life and doctrines. Schmidt's attitude was not very sympathetic. He severely condemns Suso's asceticism and blames him for doing so little to reform the abuses of the day. As a thinker he ranks him below Eckhart, Tauler and Ruysbroeck. He thinks Suso was too much of a visionary and considers his revelations to be the product of a morbid imagination. He regards him, not without cause, as the least Protestant of mediaeval mystics.

Suso's letters were edited by Preger in 1867; he believed that he had found the original text in a Munich manuscript. An acrimonious controversy ensued between Preger and Denifle, in which the latter had the best of the encounter. He showed that Preger's text was a conglomerate and that the original collection of Suso's letters made by Elsbeth Stagel was still in existence.

---

[1] See, however, Fischer, *Geschichte*, p. 13, n. 4.
[2] Herder, *Sämmtliche Werke* (ed. Suphan, 1884), 28. Band, pp. 221–225.

Denifle was particularly devoted to the great mystic, after whom he was named 'Heinrich Seuse Denifle.' In order to make Suso's works accessible to the general public, he prepared the first critical edition, in modernized German, with copious explanatory matter. One volume appeared in 1876 and the second in 1878–1880. The work proceeded slowly because of other duties, and among them the research on Eckhart, which occupied Denifle at this time.

It was incidentally Denifle who popularized the form *Seuse*, which had been already used by Pfeiffer. It goes back to the edition of 1482. Diepenbrock and Preger preferred *Suso*, which is really the Latin form of the name, employed by Surius in the sixteenth century, but dating back to the fourteenth century, for instance it was used in Suso's epitaph of 1366.[1] *Seuse* is a modern form, a variant of the mediaeval *Süs* or *Süse*. The friar was never called 'Seuse' in his own lifetime; all the oldest manuscripts have *Suse* (that is *Süse*). In English and in French he has always been called 'Suso' and I see no reason for departing from the usual practice, and this in spite of the excellent principle: 'Better to err with Pope than shine with Pye.' Englishmen can pronounce *Suso*; but one cannot trust them to tackle *Seuse* without expert guidance.

Heinrich had another name, *Amandus*, which is used in many old manuscripts, particularly those of the *Horologium*. This was adopted by him in Constance, not as his 'name in religion,' but as a cognomen or pseudonym. It was conferred on him, so to speak, in a vision by Eternal Wisdom. Unlike members of some other orders, Dominicans do not always assume a new name when they take their vows.

In the second volume of his *History of German Mysticism*, Preger gave an exhaustive account of Suso. In the matter of the transmission of the letters and other details he showed himself unrepentant, but his treatment of Suso is on the whole sympathetic and understanding.

With the appearance of Bihlmeyer's standard edition in 1907 in the original Middle High German, with a very scholarly introduction, the investigation of Suso has been placed on firm foundations. Nikolas Heller's modernized version (1926) was a retrograde step; some of the manuscripts used are defective and nothing new is added to the data of Suso's life. The annotations are, however, valuable.

During the present century a good deal of research has been carried out on Suso's vocabulary and style. This is not unnatural, because it is as a stylist and artist that he appeals most strongly to the

---

[1] The etymology from the verb *sausen*, to roar, is quite absurd, as is also that from *süss*, sweet.

literary historian. The chief names to be recorded in this connection are those of Heieck, Heyer, Nicklas and Vogt-Terhorst.

Suso's influence of mediaeval art is ably discussed by Ursula Weymann (1938). This influence was of two kinds: direct and indirect. He was himself an artist and he was fond of surrounding himself with pictures. In the chapel of the friary at Constance he had a picture of Eternal Wisdom painted on parchment; he was so attached to it that he took it with him to Cologne in his student days. He also had paintings of the Fathers of the Church with their sayings, together with symbolical figures, portrayed upon the walls. He illustrated his own works. None of the original drawings have come down to us, but there are copies in some of the oldest manuscripts[1] and in the Augsburg editions there are engravings that are ultimately derived from them.[2] The woodcuts in the 1512 Augsburg edition are attributed to Hans Burgkmair of Augsburg (1473–c. 1530). Two of these illustrations belong to *The Book of Eternal Wisdom* and ten to *The Life of the Servant*.

Apart from this direct influence on art, we must consider the results of Suso's prose which inspired artists as much as his drawings. Naturally it is not easy to differentiate between these two streams of tendency. They are both to be found in pen drawings in prayer books and devotional works, and later in woodcuts of the fifteenth and sixteenth centuries. This artistic influence is specially marked in the work of convents of the Dominican Observance in the middle of the fifteenth century. Denifle aptly calls Suso 'the Fra Angelico of mysticism.' It is interesting to note that the beautiful panel from an altar-piece in Fiesole by Fra Angelico[3] includes Suso among the Dominican saints and *beati* in paradise.

Until the beginning of the present century, the *Life* had been generally regarded as authentic, although exception had been taken to this or that detail. But in our iconoclastic age the whole work has come in for adverse criticism.[4] Attention has been drawn to the many contradictions and discrepancies in the work, which suggest that different sources were used. It is said that many passages are romantic and unhistorical, that they are not in Suso's style. The miraculous element is regarded as apocryphal. The terrible physical austerities described in the *Life* are a great stumbling-block to critics. It is alleged that this ideal of asceticism is not in accordance with the 'religion of suffering' expressed in the genuine works. If these allega-

[1] Reproduced in Bihlmeyer's edition.			[2] Reproduced in Heller's edition.
[3] In the National Gallery.
[4] Chiefly from Rieder, followed by Henri Lichtenberger and Heller.

tions are true, the book must be regarded as the work of a hagiographer or apologist, whose aim was to glorify Suso and his convent. It would then follow that the *Prologue* must be fictitious, since it states distinctly that Suso and Elsbeth Stagel were the authors.

As regards the contradictions, these need not be taken too seriously. The aim of the writer or compiler was not to produce authentic history, but a devotional book describing the religious life in all its phases. For this purpose he (or she) drew freely on Suso's life. The interpolated anecdotes are like illustrations; they have allegorical value and are not necessarily to be taken quite literally. If Suso was the author, he was perfectly free, writing as he did in the third person, to use his poet's privilege to embellish these stories, to give dramatic force or point to them. Similarly, Elsbeth Stagel might quite well idealize her hero in the portions that come from her pen. However much these tales were coloured by the imagination of the author or authors, one feels that they may be substantially true.

The argument about the miraculous element is more cogent. But here again, we must make allowances for mediaeval usage and poetic licence. It is quite correct to say that there are few miracles in *The Book of Eternal Wisdom* and none at all in *The Book of Truth*. But this is irrelevant: the difference lies in the nature of the three works concerned. A text-book of speculative mysticism expressed in terms of scholastic philosophy does not leave room for such experiences as are treated in the *Life*. We might as well look for poetry in a treatise on Algebra. *The Book of Eternal Wisdom* served purely practical ends and was written for a certain kind of public. The anecdotes in the *Life* were, in the first instance, intended for one reader only. It cannot be doubted that Suso believed in miracles as an everyday occurrence. He accepted without question the idea of continual divine intervention in his daily life. Every day, when he said mass, the consecrated host, was, as he believed, transformed into the body of Christ. This would surely be to him a much more extraordinary fact than anything mentioned in the biography.

Would he have confided these very personal things to a correspondent? The question is linked up with that of the self-inflicted mortifications. Are they credible, and if so, would a man such as Suso tell an impressionable nun about them? Would a man whom we know to be modest and self-effacing to a fault, have boasted about his hair shirt and all the rest? Did he not forbid Elsbeth to mortify the flesh? One fails to see why he should not have told his 'spiritual friend' of such matters. He made it clear to her that each person must bear his or her own cross, that some were called to asceticism and others not. It would not be difficult to impress upon her that her way was not his way. To comfort her in her illness and great pain he might easily have spoken to her of his own sufferings in the past, perhaps the distant past.

One hesitates to dismiss the *Life* as an invention. It is full of words, phrases, idioms that are thoroughly characteristic of Suso. There are such interjections as *Wafen, Eia,* images drawn from chivalry, nature scenes. We are repeatedly reminded of other passages of undisputed genuineness in the other works. If the *Life* was written by a friar in Strasbourg or by a nun at Töss, he or she must have been first a genius, and secondly thoroughly versed in Suso's tricks of thought and point of view. Moreover there are many little touches that could never have been invented by a conventional hagiographer. Suso is not invariably depicted as victorious over difficulties and temptations. He is not always heroic, sometimes just the reverse. He is a saint but a very human one. There are hesitations in his conduct, doubts in his mind, that an apologist would have deleted if he knew his job at all.

In conclusion one might say that nothing has as yet been brought forward that would invalidate the statements made in the *Prologue* of the *Life*. However ingenious the arguments of the critics, they do not carry conviction. The reliability of the *Prologue* of the *Letters* is fully confirmed by a study of the two collections, the longer one and the selection of eleven derived from it. This being so, can we reject out of hand the evidence of the general *Prologue*? One can say with confidence that the bulk of the *Life* was written in its present form by Suso or Elsbeth Stagel and it is a genuine production.[1]

[1] This view is held by Bihlmeyer, Senn and Gröber.

CHAPTER V

RULMAN MERSWIN AND THE FRIENDS OF GOD

FOR a couple of centuries the Merswin family played a prominent part in the life of the city of Strasbourg. We find them in the employment of the municipality or the bishop, benefactors of churches and monasteries, or inmates of religious houses. The best-known member of the family was Rulman Merswin, a wealthy banker and merchant. He was a man of the world, cheerful, sociable, popular and shrewd.

After the death of his first wife he married a widow named Gertrud, the daughter of a local knight. She is described as 'an honourable, simple Christian woman.' In 1347, when he was forty years old, Rulman decided, together with his wife, to renounce the world. About this time he made Tauler his confessor, and kept up a correspondence with Heinrich von Nördlingen, Margareta Ebner and other religious persons. Merswin and his wife obtained an indulgence from Pope Clement VI in 1350. There is no further definite information about him until 1367, in which year he bought from the Benedictines of Altdorf the ruined abbey of Grüner Wörth near Strasbourg. First he took over the site on a hundred years' lease; a few months later he purchased it from the Benedictines. Modern research has shown that with the astuteness of a successful business man he drove a hard bargain with the impoverished monks of Altdorf.[1]

Merswin had the monastery restored at his own expense. It was enlarged and reopened as a refuge for 'all honourable men, clergymen or laymen, knights or squires,' on condition that they defrayed their own expenses and did not molest or disturb the resident priests and brothers. Secular priests, Austin friars, Cistercians, and Dominicans applied in turn for the ownership of the house, but in vain. In 1371 it was presented to the Knights of St. John of Jerusalem, together with an annuity of fifty pounds in Strasbourg *Pfennige*. Merswin took his residence at Grüner Wörth and stayed there for the rest of his life.

The nominal head of the house was the Commander of the Knights of St. John. But he had to render an account annually to three

[1] C. Rieder, *Der Gottesfreund vom Oberland.*

trustees or guardians (Pfleger). One was the donor, Rulman Merswin, another his brother Johann, and the third a local knight named Heintzemann Wetzel. No one could be admitted without the consent of the trustees or before attaining the age of twenty. The appointment of priests depended on the nomination of the triumvirate. The final decision in all matters of importance rested with them, that is to say, with Rulman Merswin. Till his death on July 18, 1382, he remained the virtual head of the community at Grüner Wörth. Even the episcopal authority was practically eliminated, partly by legal contract, partly by reason of the exemption enjoyed by the knights of St. John.

Merswin had expended large sums, but he did not give away the rest of his fortune; he retained it under his control. In 1380 he removed to a small private house near the monastery, in order to devote himself undisturbed to religion. A few months before his death he wrote down on wax tablets his final admonitions to the community. He was buried in the church beside his second wife.

Merswin wrote many treatises and other works, but during his lifetime they were not made known to the public. They were kept in a sealed casket which was not opened till his death. Only one of these works, *Of the Four Years of His Beginning* (Von den vier Jahren seines Anfangs), is autobiographical. It deals with his decision to leave the world and devote himself to religion and good works, his early spiritual struggles, and of his meeting the Friend of God who came to see him from the Oberland.

The description of Merswin's conversion will serve as a specimen of his prose, with its endless repetitions and ponderous banality. It may be compared with the passage from Suso in the preceding chapter, which is on a similar theme. One passage carries conviction, the other raises doubts. On St. Agnes' Day Suso felt as if his soul left his body. Merswin does one better, he was not merely lifted up, he was carried bodily all round the garden many times; and a Strasbourg patrician was no featherweight! Except for this astonishing feat of levitation (which may be just a rhetorical flourish), there is nothing inherently improbable in Merswin's narrative.

'The time was just before St. Martin's Day,' he writes. 'I chanced to be alone one evening, walking in my garden, and I had a great desire to pray, and as I was thus walking about, very many thoughts came into my mind. I thought much of the falseness of the ungrateful world, and how she rewards men, and what a sore, bitter end she gives. I also came to think of the great gift that God had given me and the great love He had shown me, poor sinner, through His great suffering and His bitter death. Many such sweet and good thoughts kept coming into my mind concerning the great gift God had given me. On the other hand I thought and pondered to myself how very foolishly and vainly I had spent my life, and how very little love I had shown to God all my days. While I reflected on my little love and reflected on the great love which He had shown me here, when He lived in this wretched world in human form, while I thought of my little love and my wasted life, and that compared with His, it was as nothing, as these thoughts and many others came to me, then these thoughts became so strong that great, strong remorse rose up in me for all my wasted life. Then also I hated my own self-will very much, through which self-will I had sinned greatly and wasted my life. And as I thus walked in my garden, I looked up to heaven and called upon the unbounded mercy of God with great earnestness and with a heart full of repentance. I surrendered to God my self-will and vowed also that whatever ready money might fall to me in future I should give away for the sake of God. And as I was thus walking in the garden, simply in these thoughts and in this state of mind, it happened that a very swift, sudden, clear light came and surrounded me and I was taken and led in some manner, hovering above the ground, often round and round the garden. I was taken round about therein and some passing sweet words were spoken to me. But what the light was and the taking round and the sweet words, I do not know. God knows it, indeed, for it was quite beyond my understanding. But when this glad short hour was over, and I came to myself again, I found myself alone, standing in the garden and looking around. I found nothing new, save this one thing: I found that my eyes were flowing with tears quite involuntarily.'[1]

Merswin tells us that he used to scourge himself till the blood flowed and then rubbed salt in the wounds, as Suso did. He chose Tauler as his confessor, doubtless after hearing him preach. 'And he found out something about my austerities, for he noticed that I had become very weak, and he feared for my life and ordered me on my obedience not to practise austerities any longer. He fixed a time-limit and I had to obey ... but when the time was past I was silent and took to my austerities again more than ever before.'

Grievous temptations afflicted him at this time: first it was sensuality that troubled him and then religious doubt. He could not

---

[1] *Schriften aus der Gottesfreund-Literatur*, ed. Strauch, 2. Heft, pp. 3–5.

believe the doctrine of the Holy Trinity. His doubts tortured him so much that he feared he was doomed to eternal damnation, and his health was completely shattered. One day in church he fell into a trance and had a vision: 'A very large stone was placed before me, and out of the stone three large images of men were carved . . . and over the first was written "Father," and over the second "Son," and over the third "Holy Spirit," and it seemed as if a voice spoke to me: "Now you can believe, since you have seen the stone, that it can have three persons and yet be one stone, and the three persons are of one nature and of one stone." '

Suso also had his intellectual difficulties, but he described them discreetly and intelligently. Having overcome his doubts he was able to justify his faith in a coherent manner. Merswin was no theologian. He had spent half his life in amassing wealth, and had had no time for higher education. His attempt to expound the doctrine of the Holy Trinity can only be described as grotesque.

Merswin suffered many physical and mental tribulations, which are set forth with much vague verbiage, until the fourth year after his conversion, when he was released by supernatural grace and attained final peace. The last part of the autobiography treats, *inter alia*, his converse with the Friend of God from the Oberland. Merswin and his mysterious visitant became intimate friends. Rulman confided in the stranger all his experiences in the last four years, and at his command committed them to writing, much against his will, we are told. In exchange he received from the Friend of God the story of the latter's conversion. Complete secrecy was promised on both sides.

Among the various works that bear Merswin's name, the auto-biography alone is original. All the others are compilations. The method generally used is that of copying out a treatise of an edifying nature and interlarding it with commonplace remarks and a good deal of padding. The Knights of St. John at Grüner Wörth were well aware that Merswin had mixed up his own work and that of others, but they explained it as being due to his 'deep humility.' He did not want his own productions to be known or appreciated and hence concealed them in this way.[1] One wonders whether to admire the credulity or the charity of the noble knights. Patricians of old stock are not much in the habit of hiding their light under a bushel. Possibly the founder of Grüner Wörth gained more fame by his secretiveness and 'humility' than he would have done by ostentatious boastfulness. But he may not have seen things in that light.

[1] The passage is printed in Jundt, *Histoire du panthéisme*, p. 211, n. 1.

Even *The Book of the Nine Rocks* (Neunfelsenbuch), so long regarded as a genuine product of Merswin's pen, is now known to be an amplified version of an older treatise by an unknown author. Even the title was borrowed. The original work was badly constructed and was not improved by the process of editing at Grüner Wörth. It has been preserved in its original form and is to be found in printed editions of Suso's works that appeared in the sixteenth century and in Diepenbrock's modernized version.

It is written in dialogue form and begins with an invocation of Eternal Wisdom, which at once reminds us of Suso and partly explains why the work came to be ascribed to him. The central idea is that of a huge mountain with nine rocks or precipices. At the foot of the mountain mankind is caught in the net of sin. Few manage to extricate themselves from the net and climb the lowest rock, still fewer reach the higher ones, and on the highest there are scarcely three persons. The nine rocks symbolize the nine stages of the road to perfection. On the lowest are those who guard against mortal sin, but are without love; on the second are those who are still hampered by self-love; on the third men are devoted to spiritual exercises, but the devil has laid a snare for them, for they take pleasure in these exercises. On the highest level are those who are freed from sin and selfishness. The light of grace shines from them, unknown to themselves. They look into the source of all things.

The author of the treatise did not possess the ability to develop this scheme consistently. In the first chapter he describes how he came to write the book by divine command and how reluctant he was to do so because of his feeling of unworthiness. In the second there is an account of a vision which resembles that of the nine rocks sufficiently to be confusing, apart from being entirely superfluous. The main theme is not mentioned till the fourth chapter, in which the mountain is described, but the meaning is not explained. Then the author forgets all about the nine rocks, and in seventeen chapters he passes in review all the classes of mankind, clergy and laity, arranged in hierarchical order. With each class he enumerates the besetting sins of that class without any skill or individualization. He never gets beyond vague generalities. Thus he says that emperors and empresses, kings and queens used to be humble, obedient and conscious of their responsibilities. Now they are the reverse. The statement is not amplified in any way. Dukes, barons and freemen and their wives are proud and vain, and oppressive to the poor, unlike their forebears. Knights and squires are immodest in their dress and absurd in their bearing. They have lost all fear of God and knightly discipline. Burghers and merchants are full of avarice and vie with one another in their pride and ostentation. Artisans are full of envy and hatred. Peasants live like cattle and are full of pride, cunning, and malice. These bald statements and superficial characterizations betray the amateur. They may be contrasted with the detailed descriptions of that great moralist, Berthold von Regensburg, who knew the trade tricks of every type of merchant, and the besetting sins of lords and ladies, as only a Franciscan friar could know them.

This, then, was the work that Merswin set about to edit. As an allegory it is feeble; as literature it is puerile. Most of his additions are mere verbiage, *vox et praeterea nihil.* For example, in the prologue the fourth chapter is thus summarized in the original: 'How he saw a high mountain with nine rocks.' Merswin makes of this: 'That this man was allowed to see a very dreadful, great, high mountain with nine rocks.' But there are interpolations that are independent. The most interesting of these is a defence of Jews and pagans.[1] Written as it was at a time of anti-Semitic outbreaks, it testifies to Merswin's tolerance.

He maintains that God now loves some Jews and pagans more than many Christians. A Jew or pagan who believes his own creed to be the best, but would be prepared to give it up for a better one, is a better man than a Christian who has received baptism, but thwarts the will of God. Both Scripture and the Christian creed teach that no one can be saved except through baptism, but God will not allow a good pagan or Jew to be lost. They will be baptized in their death.

Another digression answers the question: Are there enough *Gottesfreunde* on earth to save mankind? There were only twelve Apostles, but they went out into the whole world to preach the Gospel. Merswin reveals his interest in confession. He condemns the laxity of priests who pander to the weakness of their penitents. He also castigates those Christians who often neglect communion for years, putting it off till their death-bed and thus running the risk of eternal damnation.

Merswin's other works are not of great importance. The *Little Book of the Banner* admonishes men to flee to Christ's banner and to shun that of Lucifer, which has just been unfurled. It is thought that the reference is to the Brethren of the Free Spirit. *The Book of the Three Awakenings* (Das Buch der drei Durchbrüche) tells of 'a learned and rich priest who was converted from a worldly life and

[1] Pp. 61–63.

became a sanctified devout *Gottesfreund*. He admonished and greatly improved Meister Eckhart.' This treatise has already been mentioned in an earlier chapter.[1] The situation is exactly the same as in the *Meisterbuch*, the spurious autobiography of Tauler, except that in the latter it is the layman who brings about the conversion of the priest, and in *The Book of the Three Awakenings* it is a priest who leads a great theologian and scholar to the light. Finally, Merswin produced a mystical work in which he embodied two chapters from Ruysbroeck's *Spiritual Marriage*.

Enough has been said to show that Merswin's style is loose, long-winded and tedious in the extreme. Both in what he writes of his own and in what he copies from others (which far exceeds the former), he reveals himself as unlearned, illogical, incoherent and totally lacking in discretion. What is good from the literary point of view is borrowed textually from Tauler, Suso, Albertus Magnus and others. Whole pages are taken over with but slight alterations and without any acknowledgment. Where he modifies his text it is generally to spoil it by cumbersome repetitions. He has few ideas of his own, and is not even capable of assimilating those of others without grossly exaggerating or distorting them. He reads better in English or French translation than in his native Strasbourg dialect, so that those who do not know the original tend to overestimate him.

His favourite topic is the corruption of mankind. No class, clerical or lay, is immune. Few men lead exemplary lives, the overwhelming majority are evil. They are led astray by Pharisees, or false teachers, who are skilled in the learning of the schools, but have no love of God in their hearts. They give no heed to the true *Gottesfreunde*, who alone can help them. These are the pillars of Christendom. How are they to be recognized? They are anonymous; they 'have lost their names.' They alone know the way of salvation. The phrase 'to lose their names' comes from Eckhart.[2] The remaining ideas are all to be found in Tauler's sermons, which Merswin had every opportunity of hearing. But in Tauler they form part of a sane, balanced view of human life and destiny. In his pupil they are vulgarized and simplified. What was profound in its proper context becomes crude, trivial, superficial.

How does it come about that a man of such mediocre ability should acquire a reputation in literary history? Writers on mysticism such as R. A. Vaughan, Rufus M. Jones, Evelyn Underhill, quote him frequently and with evident approval. Doubtless his plagiarism has

---

[1] See above, page 11.   [2] See Denifle, *Die Dichtungen Rulman Merswins*, pp. 523–524.

not been detected. The borrowed plumes are occasionally bright. But there is another reason for his fame. Merswin was surrounded by an air of mystery, and was not unsuccessful in creating the impression that he was a great man. Much of this was due to his supposed connection with the Friend of God in the Oberland.

Merswin informs us in his autobiography that he first met the Friend of God four years after his conversion, that is in 1351. They became firm friends and later corresponded with each other. The Friend of God also wrote to other inmates of Grüner Wörth[1] and sent copies of his works to Merswin. No less than seventeen of his writings were preserved in the library of Grüner Wörth.[2] For some thirty years no one but Merswin knew of them. About four years before his death he decided to disclose the secret, so we are told. His conscience gave him no peace; he no longer dared to conceal from his fellow-men and especially from his brethren, the Knights of St. John, such valuable productions and 'fruits of grace.' So he wrote down everything on wax tablets (strangely enough none of these has ever been discovered), deleting some names of places and persons. He then burnt the originals, both of the works of the *Gottesfreund* and of his own, because he was anxious that no one should know 'what an exceptional, sanctified, enlightened, secret, great Friend of God he (Merswin) had been.'

The community at Grüner Wörth believed implicitly in the existence of the *Gottesfreund im Oberland*. Had they not seen his letters and received his messages from Rulman Merswin? Was he not the spiritual friend of their revered founder and patron? Their curiosity was aroused by the veil of mystery that concealed him from prying eyes. Nikolaus von Löwen wrote to ask if he might join him as a disciple. Some of the other brothers at Grüner Wörth are said to have set out in search of him, visiting various friaries and other religious houses where saintly men were known to live. Merswin asserted that they had enjoyed the hospitality of the *Gottesfreund* for one night without knowing it.[3] No doubt he enjoyed the joke!

If we are to believe the records of Grüner Wörth, the influence of the *Gottesfreund* extended over a large part of Central Europe. He had many fervent disciples in the Netherlands. There were other groups in Lorraine and Hungary. His chief field of operations was the Rhine Valley and Switzerland, but he had numerous adherents in Italy, chiefly in Milan, Genoa and Rome. He was the spiritual adviser of

---

[1] For this correspondence see Strauch, *Rulman Merswin*, p. 220.
[2] For details see Strauch, p. 207; Krebs, *Merswin*, p. 360.
[3] Karl Schmidt, *Nicolaus von Basel*, pp. 62–63.

two recluses at Verona named Ursula and Adelheid. He even had a convert among the Moslems. Great was his prestige; his authority was unquestioned. Although a layman, he corresponded on equal terms with heads of religious houses and the Vicar-General of the Bishop of Strasbourg. He prophesied future events. Occasionally he emerged from the impenetrable obscurity of his Alpine hermitage to visit the outside world and influence the course of events. In 1377 he went to Rome and had an audience with the Pope. On Good Friday, 1380, a wonderful letter fell from the sky in the presence of the *Gottesfreund* and thirteen of his companions. After reading it, they saw it taken up to heaven in flames.[1] This letter, which was written in various languages, promised that in answer to their prayers and vows, a threatened calamity which would destroy the greater part of mankind would be postponed for three years. When the papal schism broke out in 1389, it seemed to confirm the apocalyptic warnings of the seer.

When Merswin was on his death-bed, the brothers asked him to confide in them the whereabouts of the messenger named Ruprecht, who had brought letters to and from the Friend of God. Merswin said that the messenger had died not long ago. So the founder of Grüner Wörth took the secret with him to the grave. After his death the quest was resumed. A pious knight and a young burgher searched for four weeks without success. In 1389 Nikolaus von Löwen was sent officially by the Knights of St. John to see Johann von Bolzenheim, Prior of the Abbey of Engelberg, who was supposed to be in touch with the mysterious Friend of God. Surely the lovely Alpine village of Engelberg would be a suitable haunt for a holy man, so remote it is from the outside world. Not only was the Prior unable to give any information, he had perforce to join in the search himself, but without achieving any result. In the following year Heinrich von Wolfach, the former Commander of the Knights of St. John at Grüner Wörth, who had exchanged letters with the *Gottesfreund*, followed up a clue that led to Klingenau in the Canton of Aargau, but failed to reach his goal.[2]

For five centuries the mystery remained unsolved. Modern scholars grappled with it manfully, attempting to discover the name of the *Gottesfreund* and to locate his hiding-place. The first theory identified him with Nikolaus von Basel, a layman who propagated Beghard tenets in Basel and the Rhine Valley, and was burnt with some companions at Vienna about 1395, after being convicted of

---

[1] Ibid., pp. 333–340. Fortunately the *Gottesfreund* secured a copy.   [2] Ibid., pp. 63–65.

heresy. This solution of the problem was quickly disposed of: it was shown that the evidence brought forward was quite inadequate. Further, the *Gottesfreund* was undoubtedly orthodox, however eccentric he may have been. He never wished to attack, still less to overthrow, the Church as he knew it. His quarrel was with individuals not with the system.

The Friend of God came from 'the Oberland.'[1] This suggested that he was a Swiss. He was, moreover, said to live in the territory of the Duke of Austria, to whom Switzerland nominally belonged. There was a good deal of wild speculation on the subject. One suggestion was that he lived at Hergiswil, on the Lake of Lucerne, at the foot of Mount Pilatus. Other theories located him at Ganterschwil in Toggenburg, or in the parish of Entlebuch in the Canton of Lucerne, or in the ancient city of Chur. All these guesses, for they were nothing more, were easily refuted.

With inexorable logic Denifle exposed the story as fictitious. The *Gottesfreund im Oberland* never existed except in the imagination of his creator. But, as so often happens, long after serious scholars had abandoned the idea, uncritical writers continued to perpetuate the legend of the 'invisible pope of an invisible church.' Let us state the case against the *Gottesfreund* as a real person as briefly as possible.

The scribes of Grüner Wörth attributed two works now to Merswin, now to the *Gottesfreund*.[2] Many writings are attributed to the latter merely on the strength of their title or prologue. There may be no internal evidence for this at all, no reference to the Friend of God, but perhaps one of the characters is called 'the man,' 'the layman,' or 'a Friend of God.' The distinction is important. A work by *a* holy man is not necessarily a work by *the* holy man. Several treatises contain the names of Merswin or the *Gottesfreund*, but the sources from which they are derived lack these names. In other words, these names were added arbitrarily by the compiler.

There are many contradictions in the data about the *Gottesfreund*. One treatise says that his conversion took place in 1342, according to two other works it was in 1339 or later. One account tells us that it was in the morning, another mentions the evening. Some treatises say that he never committed mortal sin, others that he had, and specify details. Surely the Friend of God would not make mistakes in such important details. We cannot get a clear conception of the Friend of

---

[1] An English writer is more specific, he came from the Bernese Oberland!
[2] The *Zweimannenbuch* and the *Meisterbuch*.

God from his supposed writings. Everything is vague and unconvincing.

In two letters purporting to be written by the Friend of God there are references to his journey to Rome. We gather that he travelled in a carriage, and that the date of the journey was the spring of 1377. The time taken was ten days. Historians have expressed grave doubts of the physical possibility of such a performance, especially after the severe winter of 1376. The writer of the letters seems to have had no conception of the distance from the north of Switzerland to Rome, or of the difficulties of the route over the Alps. There is a description of an interview with Gregory XI, in which the *Gottesfreund* urges the Pope to reform the Church, and threatens that if Gregory does not follow his advice, his death will speedily ensue, which event we are told, took place. This looks suspiciously like a prophecy after the event. The description of the Pope does not correspond at all to contemporary impressions.

It is curious that Merswin never allowed anyone else to see the *Gottesfreund*, to know where he lived, or even to see the messenger Ruprecht. It is also strange that Merswin allowed the *Gottesfreund* to disappear before his own demise, thus covering up all traces. He had already destroyed much of the available evidence, if it ever existed. The story of Margaretha von Kenzingen's visit, by which time the *Gottesfreund* was a hundred years old, is a later fabrication.[1]

Once we recognize the motive for the deception, the whole problem becomes clear. The Friend of God asked the Commander at Grüner Wörth to see to it that Merswin did not fast too rigorously in Lent because of the precarious state of his health. The Friend of God himself had not fasted since All Saints' Day. Does it not look as if Merswin, accustomed as he was to good living, found fasting very irksome and wanted a pretext for dispensing with it? When Merswin and the Commander could not agree about the plans for the rebuilding of the monastery, they consulted the *Gottesfreund*. First of all he agreed with the Commander, then he wrote soon afterwards to say that a new plan had been given to him by divine revelation. This was in the main the same as Merswin's. We are compelled to the conclusion that the founder of Grüner Wörth was a man who liked to have his own way, and was clever enough to think of new and strange devices for getting it. It was at the advice of the *Gottesfreund* that Merswin retired to a house of his own in the precincts, after

[1] See Denifle, in *Zeitschrift für deutsches Altertum*, 24 (1880), p. 521, note 1.

living with the Knights of St. John. The advice was no doubt very opportune.

The invention of the Friend of God and his small community of pious men who directed the spiritual welfare of a host of religious persons united by a secret tie, was a grandiose conception. But Merswin was not intelligent enough to carry it out consistently. The letters are particularly suspect; they are full of discrepancies. The dates are unreliable. Many letters cited are not in existence and probably never did exist.

Apart from passages that are taken over bodily, or with slight modification, from other sources, the work of the Friend of God is on the same literary level as that of Rulman Merswin. It is written in the same long-winded style; it contains the same thoughts or lack of thought, the same *clichés* and pet phrases, the same sentimentality. Parts of Merswin's *Book of the Nine Rocks* correspond word for word with parts of *The Spiritual Ladder* (Die geistlichen Staffeln) by the *Gottesfreund*. It is true that there are some differences between individual works. *The Book of the Five Men* has a different spelling and is in a different dialect from Merswin's treatises. But the language of the former does not resemble any known dialect of German and is obviously a synthetic form of speech, with a perfectly absurd orthography. With his usual directness, Denifle does not hesitate to use the word 'forgery.' The difference in handwriting would not deceive anyone who looked below the surface. To write a manuscript labelled 'in the *Gottesfreund's* own hand' and invent a new kind of spelling and a disguised hand, was all part of the game of mystification. Even the miraculous letter from heaven sent to the *Gottesfreund*, is a typical specimen of Merswin's prose.

The great majority of those who are competent to judge accepted Denifle's closely reasoned argument that the *Gottesfreund* was a fictitious person.[1] Most scholars agreed with Denifle that Merswin was the author of the deception.[2] As this was inconsistent with the view that Merswin was a mystic and a pious man, a variant of the theory was enunciated.[3] Nikolaus von Löwen now becomes the culprit. He was a scribe from Flanders, Löwen being the equivalent of Louvain. As a result of the close commercial ties between Strasbourg and the Low Countries, Nikolaus obtained a post in Strasbourg and later became Merswin's secretary. At Grüner Wörth he

---

[1] Die Dichtungen Rulman Merswins, pp. 527–540.
[2] The one exception was Preger who remained impenitent. Jundt, at first unconvinced, later capitulated.
[3] By Karl Rieder.

took holy orders and joined the Order of St. John of Jerusalem, after serving in the church of the community for four years as a secular priest. This new theory exculpates Rulman Merswin, but it has the disadvantage of making Nikolaus not only the author of all the works attributed to the *Gottesfreund*, but also of those that bear the name of Merswin. In order to solve one problem, the author of this hypothesis creates new difficulties. The motive of the forgeries is said to be to glorify Grüner Wörth and its founder. This theory has not received much support. Denifle's explanation still holds the field.

A third supposition[1] attempts to rehabilitate Merswin, while still holding him responsible for the invention of the shadowy figure of the *Gottesfreund*. According to this view, Merswin had a split personality. One part of him was the astute business man who became the pious benefactor, the other was a visionary who had hallucinations, among which was the existence of the *Gottesfreund*. In order to save Merswin's integrity, his sanity is sacrificed. This is a charitable view, but unfortunately there is nothing to support it.

Must we then go the whole hog and stamp Merswin as an impostor? Nikolaus von Löwen, who as far as one can judge, was an inoffensive and rather credulous man, tells us that during Merswin's lifetime no one knew what a great saint he was. This may have been due to Merswin's modesty and reticence, but on the other hand, he may have been a *poseur* and a bit of a hypocrite. We have only his word for it that he practised awful austerities, suffered the most appalling temptations, from which death seemed the only release, and had visions of indescribable splendour and sweetness. Perhaps we should give him the benefit of the doubt. He was a garrulous old windbag, but that is not to say that he was a criminal. As to the invention of the *Gottesfreund*, it was not necessarily reprehensible. It is the motive that really matters. If it was a fraud, it was a pious fraud.

It can scarcely be doubted that Merswin's ambition was to maintain order and discipline in the monastery of Grüner Wörth, which was a house of the Knights of St. John, besides being a kind of charitable foundation for Strasbourg patricians. Human motives are rarely unmixed, and it would not be surprising if Merswin's idealism was mingled with a certain amount of self-interest. He certainly succeeded in his aims as far as the house itself was concerned. It became a great centre of literary production. Books were written and copied. The works of the great mystics were read and reproduced. An excellent library was built up. Even in the second half of

[1] Jundt (1890).

the fifteenth century, Grüner Wörth continued to be a very well regulated house and maintained a sound tradition.[1]

But before bidding farewell to Rulman and the Knights of St. John, we might consider the seventeen works that were ascribed to the mythical *Gottesfreund im Oberland.* The most important of these is the *Meisterbuch,* which was long regarded as the biography of Tauler. As we have already seen,[2] the 'Master' of this work cannot be Tauler, who never had that title. It is equally certain that the 'layman,' who converted the 'Master,' is only one of the many metamorphoses of the *Gottesfreund,* that is to say, he is an invention of Merswin. The work has all the well-known characteristics of Merswin's style, if we except those portions that are copied from earlier works. It is amazing that the sermons contained in this crude and clumsy production should have been so long associated with Tauler, who was a poet with a great wealth of imagery at his disposal. Tauler was, moreover, a man of discretion, and would never have told the extremely unedifying story of the adultress and her illegitimate child in a sermon, and what is more, in a sermon to nuns! Even the scribes themselves omitted it from all manuscripts save the oldest; and a mediaeval scribe was not very squeamish, as a rule.

According to the Prologue of the *Fünfmannenbuch,* or *Book of the Five Men,*[3] the brothers of Grüner Wörth wished to have something written for them by the hand of the *Gottesfreund,* and consequently he sent his dear friend Rulman Merswin a description of the inner life of his pious companions in their mountain home. But he wrote it in five days (it is not clear why he was in such a tremendous hurry) and hence mixed up the Alsatian dialect with his own. We have already seen the implications of this mixture of dialects. The *Gottesfreund* ordered Nikolaus von Löwen to copy the book out in a more legible hand. The manuscript of this work, supposedly the autograph of the *Gottesfreund,* is still in existence. It is written in Merswin's style. It tells of temptations long and severe, above all relating to unchastity and doubt (Merswin's besetting sins), of asceticism and miraculous intervention, of visions and mystical experiences. At the end the *Gottesfreund* adds a few remarks about himself: there is the usual reluctance to write anything personal. He promises that Rulman Merswin will provide additional information if he (Merswin) survives the *Gottesfreund.* We learn that Merswin knows where the complete biography of his mysterious friend is to be found, and he

[1] See Engelbert, *Krebs,* p. 367.   [2] See above, p. 43.
[3] Printed in Strauch, *Schriften,* 2. Heft, p. 28.

will make it known to the Knights of St. John at the proper time and also divulge the name of the *Gottesfreund*.

The Book of the Two Fifteen-Year Old Boys and *The Book of the Two Men*[1] are both autobiographical. In the first the Friend of God gives an account of his childhood and his conversion, together with that of his young friend. In the second the five years that followed the conversion are described. We learn that the *Gottesfreund* was the son of a rich merchant (as Merswin was), and that in his youth he went on long journeys in foreign parts. A number of religious questions are discussed in dialogue form.

Most of the works of the Friend of God are of little importance except as compilations of a type of literature that we shall have to consider shortly. Several of them are very short, running only to two or three pages of manuscript, but among the longer and more interesting ones is *The Tale of the Imprisoned Knight*.[2] This is a little romance of chivalry that is not without charm, although it is not Merswin who is responsible for this.

It was drawn from various sources and was perhaps to some extent founded on fact. It tells of two squires who were inseparable friends and shared all their joys and sorrows. They sought service together with a young baron to whom they were both devoted. They went together to Prussia to win their spurs. On their return it chanced that one of them fell ill, and in his absence the other was captured by a knight who kept him for years imprisoned in his castle. The avaricious captor demanded a huge ransom. Despite the most strenuous efforts, his friend was unable to raise the money. Escape was impossible, liberation unthinkable. In his grief and despair, the prisoner confessed his sins to God, and as there was no priest to shrive him, he called upon the Virgin to intercede on his behalf.

At midnight he saw a bright light, and heard a heavenly voice that comforted him and promised that he would be set free. He was told that the next morning, when the priest said mass in the chapel above, he would receive half of the consecrated host and his chains would fall from his feet. This took place and was repeated the next two mornings. Half a host floated into his mouth in the midst of a shining light. He felt no hunger and left untouched the loaf of bread that was given him every day. The gaoler saw the light and heard the voice, but at first he did not dare to tell the lord of the castle 'on account of his great cruelty.' But when the third day came, he

---

[1] Edited by Karl Schmidt, *Nicolaus von Basel*, and also (*Zweimannenbuch* only) by Lauchert Bonn, 1896.

[2] Karl Schmidt, *loc. cit.*, pp. 139–186.

thought it better to incur the wrath of his master rather than let the prisoner escape, 'whether by the help of God or the devil.' So the gaoler told his story and the prisoner was finally brought out of the tower.

He was asked to explain what had happened, but refused to do so until he had obtained the permission of the heavenly visitant. The captive prophesied that at the sixth hour two travellers from Lombardy would arrive at the castle. The prophecy was fulfilled, and in the presence of the knight and his household, the two strangers, the chaplain and a Franciscan friar, the prisoner told his story and was miraculously freed from his chains. Other wonders followed: the liberated captive related that the stern knight said six Aves every day to the honour of the Virgin, and that his wife often prayed to the Virgin on behalf of her husband. The lord of the castle and his family were converted. The next day they all made their confession and communicated. They intreated the prisoner to stay with them, but he declined their invitation.

On returning home he met the friend of his youth who would not talk of anything but worldly love and took no interest in religion. But after hearing the story of his old companion's adventures in the tower and his miraculous release, he too was converted and the old friendship was revived. The former prisoner communicated daily for two years. Once he stopped and was unable to take any food until the practice was resumed. For two hours daily he was in an ecstasy and felt wonderful peace and joy. He suffered, however, from grievous temptations, specially from gluttony, sensuality and doubt. He had diabolical visitations when he received the sacraments. He underwent severe physical austerities, wore a hair shirt and coat of mail continually, slept on straw, never on a bed, and avoided dainty fare. He grew in holiness, receiving much benefit from the ministrations of a *Gottesfreund*. In a trance he was relieved once and for all of his tribulations, except the temptations to unchastity, which remained till his death.

An Ariosto or a Chaucer would have made a delightful poem out of a subject like this. A bungler like Merswin could do nothing beyond watering down his original source. The mention of a Franciscan friar and a convent of Franciscan nuns in the neighbourhood of the castle is noteworthy. The two daughters of the wicked knight wanted to enter the nunnery, but their father refused to allow it. After his conversion the father asked the prisoner for his advice. On due investigation the latter advised him to let his daughters do as they wished. The knight and his wife left the castle to be used as a gaol, and went to live in the town in order to be near the Franciscan church, where they wished to attend mass and hear the sermons. All this strongly suggests a Franciscan author. A characteristic feature of the story is the strong emphasis laid on the veneration of the sacrament, the advantages of communicating frequently and the miracles wrought by the consecrated host. This is typical of the fourteenth century, and we come across it in Franciscan sermons of that time.

The theme of friendship recurs in another of these stories, *The Life of Two Holy Nuns in Bavaria*.[1] About the year 1315 two maidens, thirteen years of age, named Margareta and Katharina, vowed before the crucifix to renounce the world. They overcame the opposition of their parents and entered the convent. At one side of the dormitory two cells with a communicating door were constructed for them so that they could be together continually. They won the affection and esteem of the other sisters and for seventeen years they shared the common life of the community, but unknown to the others, they had ecstasies and mystical visions.

Once on Shrove Tuesday they were in an ecstasy and sat till Sunday rigid and motionless. Their absence was noticed in the choir; the prioress had the door opened by the smith and the two girls were found sitting there with a wreath of roses on their heads. They maintained silence on what had happened until their confessor had given them permission to speak. They lived a holy life in the convent for forty years, and after their death the priest gave the prioress the story of their experiences, which he had written down, telling of their scourgings till the blood flowed, the divine command to desist from these practices, their long periods of spiritual depression and lack of consolation, their visions, temptations to unchastity and visitations of the devil in various human forms, and their final glorification.

If the *Gottesfreund* in the singular, whose suppressed writings we have briefly surveyed, must be relegated to the realm of myth, the *Gottesfreunde* in the plural are in a different category. They actually existed, but so much nonsense has been written about them that drastic action is required to clear away the vast accumulation of legend and error.

The term 'Friend of God' is not an invention of the Middle Ages.[2] It has a long history and goes back to pre-Christian times. It occurs

---

[1] Printed by Strauch, *Schriften aus der Gottesfreund-Literatur*, 1. Heft.
[2] The best account is that of Erik Peterson.

both in the Old and New Testaments as a description of Abraham.[1]
Christ called His disciples friends,[2] and this was doubtless the chief
source of its later use. The Fathers of the Church apply the term to
Abraham, Moses, and the Apostles. Clement of Alexandria and
Chrysostom call the martyrs 'Friends of God.' Thomas Aquinas
discusses the nature of friendship and inquires under what conditions
the word can properly be applied to the relationship between God
and man.[3]

The phrase becomes popular with the German mystics. It is used
in quite a general sense by Mechthild von Magdeburg and there are
a few isolated examples in Eckhart, but it is Tauler who first uses it
frequently. It is one of his most characteristic expressions. From about
1340 onwards it becomes part of the ordinary vocabulary of the
mystics. As far as one can judge, this is due to Tauler's influence. He
apparently set the fashion during his Strasbourg and Basel periods.

In the fourteenth century *Gottesfreund* has two different meanings.
Sometimes it is equivalent to 'pious, devout person' or 'saint' in a
general sense. It is used in this way quite often of the Old Testament
Patriarchs, the Apostles, and the Virgin Mary. This is a continuation
of the patristic tradition. There is also a technical meaning of the
word. Tauler, Merswin and Marquart von Lindau distinguish
between 'true' and 'false' Friends of God. The latter were the
Brethren of the Free Spirit and heretics generally. We are not concerned with them here. The 'true' Friends of God were persons
with strong mystical tendencies and interests, and in particular those
who had attained union with God, the highest stage of the contemplative life.

They formed a kind of spiritual *élite* within the Church, and
sought to raise the general tone and level of religious life; but they
were orthodox and had no intention of forming a new sect. They
regarded the Church as the mystical Body of Christ, one and indivisible. They were not in any sense an organized society or congregation. This point cannot be too strongly emphasized. One can quite
understand how the opposite view grew up. In the seventh chapter
of the second part of the *Horologium*, Suso gave instructions to those
who wished to become Servants of Eternal Wisdom, and sketched a
scheme of devotions for such persons. This chapter was translated
into German, although not by Suso himself, under the title of
'The Brotherhood of Eternal Wisdom.' The title was invented by

---

[1] Exodus xxxiii. 11; James ii. 23.   [2] John xv. 15.
[3] *Summa Theologica*, II, ii, Quaest. 23, Art. 5; Summa contra Gentiles, IV, 54.

the unknown translator; it is not in the Latin original. Carl Schmidt overlooked this fact and jumped to the conclusion that the 'Brotherhood' was just another name for *Gottesfreunde*, and that they practised Suso's precepts as an organized body. It remains to be proved that Suso's plan was ever carried out. We do not hear of any community that called itself a 'Brotherhood of Eternal Wisdom.' Nor is it correct to identify the Brethren of the Common Life, founded by Gerhard Groot, the disciple of Ruysbroeck, as a group of Friends of God.

Preger is quite definite about the matter: 'Neither in these (the letters of Tauler, Heinrich von Nördlingen, etc.), nor in any other writings of the time do we come across statements which compel us to think of the *Gottesfreunde* as a formal society. Everywhere we find only a free association of like-minded friends with one another.'[1] It might be added that some of the *Gottesfreunde*, like Suso, were completely isolated in their convents, living among indifferent or hostile members of a religious community. Others formed part of a small circle of devout persons who shared religious proclivities. Broadly speaking, 'Friend of God' simply means 'mystic.'

It is a curious fact that Ruysbroeck[2] makes a distinction between the Friends of God and the 'secret Sons of God' (occulti filii Dei). The former have not yet reached the highest stage of perfection; they still cling to self in some measure. But the Sons of God have become liberated from the last vestiges of self-love and attained the pure love of God. This indicates that the term 'Friend of God' is sometimes used rather loosely; the terminology is not stereotyped.

The *Gottesfreunde* differed in their political opinions: most of them were partisans of the Pope, a few supported the Emperor. Christina Ebner said on occasion very harsh things about the Pope; but she is attacking an individual pontiff, not the papacy as an institution. But whatever the differences between them, the Friends of God were united by the bond of common aspirations and experiences.

There were among them Dominican friars and nuns, later also Franciscans. From the beginning the Beguines were represented, and there were also laymen among them. We come across members of most of the great religious orders. It is, however, quite incorrect to say that among them 'heretical Waldensians were just as welcome as orthodox Catholics.'[3] On the contrary, there is not the slightest evidence that the 'true' Friends of God ever associated in any way with

---

[1] *Geschichte*, II, p. 296.   [2] *De Calculo sive de Perfectione Filiorum Dei* (1692), cap. 8.
[3] E. F. Bevan, *Three Friends of God*, pp. viii, 36, p. 321.

Waldensians. This erroneous notion has sprung up because Carl Schmidt and other writers identified the *Gottesfreund im Oberland* (in whose historicity they firmly believed) with a heretic, to wit, Nikolaus von Basel.[1] The spurious *Meisterbuch* gave some colour to this erroneous belief.

Another fruitful cause of misunderstanding is the fact that in some of the treatises of the *Gottesfreunde* we read about priests who take instruction from laymen. This is taken to be evidence of the existence of a kind of mediaeval Protestantism. In the first place, the spiritual leader is not always a layman: he may be a priest, as in two of the stories printed by Strauch.[2] In the second place, it is one thing to have a deep respect for a layman or woman, even to look upon them as channels of spiritual grace, but it is quite another thing to wish to abolish the difference between clergy and laity. St. Teresa was treated with great respect by priests, but it was they who administered the sacraments to her not she to them.

Admittedly there were Friends of God who were not in holy orders. Merswin was a layman, so was Hermann von Fritzlar, a minor writer who studied at Bologna and collected or compiled lives of the saints. But no one would call such men creative personalities in the literary sphere or in that of ideas. Hermann had not an ounce of originality in him. His literary methods, even more than those of Merswin, were of the 'scissors and paste' variety.

We cannot ignore the monastic background. The majority of the active and influential Friends of God were friars, monks and nuns. Most of the men were in holy orders. They said mass daily, sang the office, preached sermons in the church, heard confessions. They invoked the Virgin Mary and the saints, prayed before the crucifix or images, observed holy days, fasted and mortified the flesh with extreme rigour. All this is absolutely axiomatic. We hear now and then of Beguine houses in which saintly women led consecrated lives, but all the outstanding female mystics were nuns in convents.

The mystery with which Rulman Merswin surrounded the *Gottesfreund im Oberland*, and also his own writings and personality, added to other factors, have given rise to the belief that the Friends of God were a secret society. There were, no doubt, groups of heretics that concealed their identity, but the 'true' Friends of God, with whom we are chiefly concerned, had no reason to fear the ecclesiastical authorities. If it is objected that Eckhart was a *Gottesfreund* and

[1] Rufus Jones (*Studies in Mystical Religion*, 1919, p. 246) is wrong in thinking that this view goes back to the fifteenth century.
[2] *Schriften*, 1. Heft.

that he was condemned for his doctrines, it might be pointed out that the 'movement,' if we can so designate it, did not begin until after Eckhart's death.

Some confusion has been caused by a passage in Tauler: 'I know a man, one of the greatest Friends of God, who has been a ploughman all his days.' There is no need to read into these words more than is actually said. Tauler knew of a ploughman (the verb in the original does not necessarily mean that he knew him personally) who was a good Christian. There is no reason to assume, as many writers have done, that the ploughman was a member of a secret organization with a strong anti-papal bias, which was persecuted by the authorities.

It is true that such men as Tauler and Merswin (who is so often Tauler's echo) use the phrase 'a secret Friend of God.' This is taken to mean that the person in question belonged to a kind of religious underground movement. What Tauler means is 'saints whose sanctity is known to God, not to men,' that is, persons hidden away in some monastery, hermitage, or for that matter, persons living in the outer world, whose good deeds are done in secret, and who are regarded as fools or eccentrics by their fellows. Such a person was Suso, who tells us that after his first ecstasy on St. Agnes' Day, his companions never noticed any difference in him or suspected that he had changed.

As regards the geographical distribution of mysticism (and hence of the Friends of God), Strasbourg was undoubtedly the great centre. Its extensive trade brought wealth; its new democratic constitution favoured the growth of ideas. Here Eckhart and Tauler preached and here Merswin founded Grüner Wörth. From this city influence radiated out in all directions, but especially northwards to Cologne, south to Basel, and up the Rhine Valley to Constance. This was the great highway of commerce; it was called the *Pfaffengasse*, or 'parsons' alley,' because it was the road to Rome, and it connected the great episcopal cities of Cologne, Strasbourg and Basel. As trade flowed north and south along the old Roman road, so also ideas pursued the same direction. It is no mere accident that we find the Waldensians in the same towns as the mystics proper. The 'false' Friends of God and the 'true' ones occupied the same territory.

The northern extension of the *Pfaffengasse* led to the Netherlands, and we find *Gottesfreunde* there also. There were strong links between Strasbourg and the monastery of Groenendal, near Waterloo, where Ruysbroeck ruled as prior. Many were the visitors who came to see the holy man and Tauler is said to have been one of them. Ruysbroeck sent a copy of his *Book of the Adornment of Spiritual Marriage* to Grüner Wörth, where it was excerpted by Merswin. There were colonies of mystics to the east and west. In the neighbourhood of Nürnberg there was the nunnery of Engeltal, and some fifty miles to the south was Maria Medingen; in Northern Switzerland there were the convents of Töss near Winterthur, Oetenbach and Zurich. There was Adelshausen near Freiburg im Breisgau, Kaisersheim in Bavaria, and finally Unterlinden at Colmar in Alsace. In all these places mystics were to be found, books were copied and written.

The Friends of God were indefatigable correspondents. Reference has already been made to the famous letters exchanged by Suso and his collaborator and biographer Elsbeth Stagel of Töss. The correspondence of Margareta Ebner at Maria Medingen and Heinrich von Nördlingen is scarcely less famous. It is the oldest collection of letters in the German language and of exceptional interest for the historian of manners and social conditions. Heinrich von Nördlingen was a secular priest, known in literary history for his excellent translation of Mechthild von Magdeburg's work *Das fliessende Licht der Gottheit* into High German. He encouraged Margareta Ebner to write down her revelations and visions, to which he attached supreme importance.

There is a whole mass of literature associated with the Friends of God as authors or compilers. It is characterized by certain recurrent themes. A sombre view is taken of the world and its wickedness. Such is the prevailing depravity that few will be saved. The only shining lights are the Friends of God, who are the pillars of Christendom. The only means of salvation is to attach oneself to one of these saintly persons and obey him implicitly 'in place of God.' Complete submission to the will of God and guidance by a recognized saint, whether an anchorite in the forest, a priest in the town, or a layman, is the unfailing mark of the true Christian. To submit involves the renunciation of one's own self-will.

Another feature is the stress laid on fasting and scourging, in fact on all kinds of bodily austerities. Intellectual pride is regarded as a great obstacle to progress. The Friends of God have little respect for learning. They consider it a snare and a delusion. Religious experience, above all union with the divine, is worth more than all the erudition or hair-splitting of the schools, which perplex men but do not promote their salvation. There is, in fact, a strong anti-intellectual tendency in the literature of the time. In the hand of a Tauler these ideas are restrained; they form part of a balanced view of man and his destiny; in other writers they tend to assume a more extreme form.

Towards the end of the fourteenth century the word *Gottesfreund* gradually disappears from use. After the early fifteenth century we no longer come across it, either because of the general decline of mysticism and of the terminology connected with it, or because the word itself fell into disrepute as a result of heretical associations. Among the last to use it were the Franciscans, of whom we shall have more to say in the next chapter.

CHAPTER VI

THE FRANCISCANS

SAINT Dominic's aim in founding an order was to combat heresy. From the very first great importance was attached to education as a means to this end. Among the Franciscans learning was a later innovation; among the Friars Preachers it was always an essential element. The peculiar organization of the Dominican Order which, by means of special dispensations, allowed some of its members to devote themselves exclusively to study and meditation, was particularly favourable to the cultivation of learning and the growth of speculation. It made possible the erection of the stately edifice of scholastic philosophy; it produced a Thomas Aquinas.

In the domain of learning the Franciscans rapidly made up the leeway. Quite early in the history of their Order they had some very eminent scholars: Adam of Marsh, Alexander of Hales and St. Bonaventura are conspicuous examples. The Friars Minor of Paris and Oxford added lustre to the annals of these two great universities. In Germany the *studium generale* of Magdeburg opened auspiciously about the year 1230, under the charge of Bartholomew the Englishman. The school of Cologne secured the services of Duns Scotus in 1307.

From the beginning of the thirteenth century the Franciscans played their part in German literature. Friar Albert at Stade and Heinrich von Burgeis in the Tyrol both composed lengthy allegorical epics. The friary of Regensburg was, however, the chief centre. It boasted a poet, Friar Lamprecht, the author of a rhymed life of St. Francis and a didactic poem entitled *Tochter Syon*. These works did not rise above the general level of contemporary verse. But Regensburg had two outstanding writers: Berthold von Regensburg and his associate David von Augsburg.[1] Berthold was the greatest German preacher of the Middle Ages; his fame was known to Roger Bacon in England and to Salimbene in Italy. From Berthold there descends an unbroken tradition of Franciscan preachers and sermon writers until the beginning of the fifteenth century.[2]

The Friars Minor had their own mystical traditions, beginning

---

[1] The best account is that of Dagobert Stöckerl.
[2] Conrad of Saxony, Ludovicus, Greculus, John of Werden (the author of *Dormi Secure*), and Johann Bischoff.

with St. Francis and continuing through St. Bonaventura, to whom Eckhart, Tauler and Suso were considerably indebted. We should therefore naturally expect that the great age of Franciscan literature in the Empire, between 1240 and 1270, when Berthold and David wrote, would coincide with the best period of Franciscan mysticism. This was not the case. The heyday of German mysticism really begins with Eckhart's activity, by which time Franciscan literature had already passed its prime.

David von Augsburg was a novice master at Regensburg and his principal work dealt with the training of novices. It was officially adopted by the Order as a text-book and enjoyed extraordinary popularity throughout the Middle Ages. In 1246 David acted as papal visitor or inspector of a nunnery at Regensburg. He died in 1272. If we are to accept the view that he was the author of *De Inquisitione Haereticorum*,[1] he acted as an inquisitor in a campaign against the Waldensians in Bavaria.

He accompanied Berthold von Regensburg on his preaching expeditions, and in the course of his wide travels as a teacher, preacher, confessor and missionary, no less than in the friary of Regensburg, he acquired that profound knowledge of human motives and emotions that is so clearly revealed in all his Latin and German works. He had a keen, critical intellect, and was trained to express himself concisely and lucidly. He knew how to develop an idea consistently, or construct a treatise logically. His vernacular writings are magnificent specimens of mediaeval prose. His style is clear, simple, forceful. He never speaks unless he has something to say, and he says it well.

While conceding to true mysticism its place in the scheme of things, its ethical value and importance, he was more concerned to point out the difficulties and snares of the mystic way than its triumphs. He must have learnt from his own observation, and he was a keen observer, the dangers of emotional religion for untrained minds. His treatment of mysticism is therefore pre-eminently intellectual. He can classify, analyse, describe, but he does so with a restraint and objectivity that have led some scholars to deny that he was a mystic at all. If, however, we include in the term those who make the striving of the human soul for rest in God and union with Him the object of their inquiry, he can properly find a place in our investigations.

His attitude is well exemplified in the Latin treatise *De Septem*

---

[1] This is the general opinion, see, however, Pelster, *Zeitschrift für katholische Theologie*, 1921, pp. 609-627.

Gradibus Orationis, of which there is a German translation under the title, *Die sieben Staffel des Gebetes* (The Seven Stages of Prayer).[1] The approach to mystical experience is by means of prayer. At first this is vocal; it requires an effort of will and concentration. In the course of time it becomes effortless and spontaneous; it is accompanied by articulate words, an inner joy. It is finally possible to pray without articulate words, which constitutes inward or mental prayer. More and more the worshipper learns to give way to the divine will instead of seeking his own. The sixth stage is known as 'mystic sleep' and the next is union with God, the highest state realizable here on earth. The seventh and final phase is the beatific vision in heaven, in which 'the mirror is completely taken away through which we see God here, in which we are completely like God and see Him face to face, just as He is.'

Such phrases as the last are liable to be interpreted in a pantheistic sense. To guard against such misunderstandings, David strongly stressed the fact that in the highest stages of contemplation a humble childlike attitude is essential,[2] that we are children of God by adoption, not by nature, and that there must always be an infinite gulf between God and man.

David charts out the mystic way; he is familiar with all its well-known phases: jubilation, intoxication of the spirit (ebrietas), spiritual joy (jucunditas), dissolution (liquefactio), and defines them with scriptural and patristic examples. He devotes a special chapter[3] to the 'dark night of the soul,' in which the worshipper feels himself to be forsaken by God; his heart is dry and arid; even Holy Communion gives no consolation. David tells us that this is not to be regarded as a trial imposed on us; in many cases it is just due to tiredness after the exhausting efforts of the pursuit of inward perfection, not to speak of asceticism. The only effective method of curing it is either wise submission or complete rest.[4]

Following Augustine,[5] David distinguishes three kinds of visions: corporeal, imaginative, and intellectual.[6] He further sub-divides the second class into two groups: waking and sleeping visions. By corporeal revelation he understands that in which the physical eye sees a visible object or the physical ear hears a spoken word. In the imaginative visions it is the inner eye, the eye of the mind that functions. The intellectual revelations refer to abstract ideas rather than to con-

[1] Edited by Pfeiffer, *Deutsche Mystiker*, I, 387–397.   [2] Pfeiffer, I, 367.
[3] *De Septem Processibus*, c. 64, pp. 347–351.   [4] Ibid., c. 69, pp. 367–373.
[5] *De Genesi ad Litteram*, lib. XII, c. 6, 7, 8 (Migne, *Patrologia Latina*, 34, pp. 458–460).
[6] *De Septem Processibus*, p. 346.

crete objects. The truth is perceived by the human reason. As St.
Teresa puts it, without seeing anything, the spirit conceives its object.

David now deals with what we might call the abnormal symptoms
of mysticism and he gives a word of warning. In the sphere in which
the natural and the supernatural meet, the dangers of self-deception
are very great. 'Some persons may find the truth in revelations,
visions and apparitions, but most are deceived. We shall therefore
not dwell long on these phenomena. Those who know them are
frequently led astray and even if their experiences are genuine, their
real value is slight. It is true that the illiterate and those who
are ignorant of spiritual charismata believe that there is in them a
clear proof of special holiness and wisdom.'[1]

While carefully distinguishing between pure and lascivious visions,
David sternly condemns the intrusion of the erotic element into
religion. The passage exemplifies his objective, matter-of-fact, un-
emotional approach to the subject. 'We believe that Christ is in
heaven in His glorified body and is no longer here in reality being
born of the Virgin, or nursed by her, or suffering, or doing anything
else that He did according to the account of the Gospel during His
bodily life here on earth among men. And yet it is often reported that
He has shown Himself to some holy and pious persons in His Nativity,
on in His Mother's womb, or extended on the cross, not as if it had
really been happening, but because He wished to appear in this way
as a special consolation to them to arouse their devotion or for some
other spiritual reason.'[2]

He goes on to say that this is equally true of apparitions of saints
and angels, and continues: 'I think I cannot pass over in silence the
fact that some, deceived by evil spirits or by their own false opinions,
think that Christ and the glorious Mother of God appear to them
and not only bestow on them kisses and embraces, but even more
unseemly gestures and actions, so that just as their spirit is inwardly
comforted, the flesh is outwardly caressed. That this is not only
deception and seduction, but gross blasphemy is evident. For the
Holy Spirit is poured out in order to combat and suppress all passions
and particularly the lusts of the flesh. If the spirit of purity sheds its
splendour anywhere, all passions and sensual desire must immediately
cease and disappear as the darkness on the approach of light.'[3]

David's strictures were by no means isolated. We have some reason
to think that they were typical of the attitude of the Regensburg
friary, for the poet Lamprecht spoke scornfully of the mystical nuns

[1] Ibid. [2] Ibid. [3] Ibid., pp. 359–360.

of Brabant and Bavaria. There were, however, other Franciscan centres where mystical problems were studied and discussed. We might, for example, consider the anonymous writer of a sermon in a Bodleian manuscript.[1] He was a lector in a Franciscan friary in the second half of the thirteenth century. That is all we know about him. The *thema*, or as we should say, the text, of the sermon is 'Behold, I make all things new.'[2] But as in Eckhart's sermons, there is no connection between the text and the subject treated.

The friar wishes to expound a mystical doctrine and the text is just a peg on which to hang his remarks. It is true that the sermon is divided into four parts, corresponding to the four words of the *thema*: *Ecce, nova facio omnia*, but this division is artificial and arbitrary. The *propositio* is 'How can the soul attain union with the blessed?' The sermon is much abridged, as is natural, because it is meant for devotional reading, not as a model for preachers. Some links in the argument are missing, so that there is occasional obscurity.

The substance of the four sections is as follows: (1) in order to attain union with the saints in heaven, the soul must imitate them here in this life, since nothing unites so much as similarity. We cannot deserve to know God by any external action; only rational actions can lead us to Him. If we use our reason we can recognize God in all things. The more we die to ourselves the more we shall know God. (2) The saints in eternal life have everything new and fresh, because there is nothing in heaven that can make them old. Those who wish to have eternal life must always be fresh, must always be on their guard against lukewarmness and idleness. Continual effort is needed for the upward progression of the soul. (3) The chief activity of the blessed is love. In this life we can never know love fully. In order to know a thing fully, we must know its cause and its purpose. God alone is the proper object of love, and as no one can fully know what God is, no one can fully know what love is. Through the union of love, man becomes godlike (gotvar). The blessed in eternal life do almighty works because it is not they who act, but God in them. (4) God is in all things, and those who seek to follow Him should not take anything as it is *per se*, but should seek God in all things, and seek all things only in so far as they bear them towards God. With some reflections on the nature of the Deity the sermon ends.

The unknown writer was familiar with scholastic philosophy. He quotes Dionysius the Pseudo-Areopagite on God as darkness, and

---

[1] *Laud Misc.* 479. Edited by Strauch, *Deutsche Texte des Mittelalters*, Band XXX, 1919.
[2] Revelation xxi. 5.

Bonaventura on God as the centre of a sphere whose circumference is everywhere.[1] He has German equivalents for many abstract Latin terms and this work illustrates the manner in which the German mystics created a philosophical vocabulary in the vernacular. It is, however, a mistake to call him a pupil of Eckhart.[2] It is quite evident that he was trained in the Franciscan tradition, for he says that love is the highest activity of the blessed. The Dominican scribe of the manuscript protests: 'The friars and lectors in the Order of Preachers do not accept a teaching that he sets out when he says that the highest and greatest activity of the blessed in heaven is love. It is knowledge, say the Preachers, and they are right, for Christ said: "This is eternal life, that they might know Thee, the only true God and Jesus Christ, whom Thou hast sent." '[3]

This is an allusion to a controversy between the two Orders. The Dominican scribe just quoted gives us the official doctrine of the Friars Preachers, as laid down by Thomas Aquinas. Duns Scotus opposed this; he gave the precedence to the will, not the intellect, maintaining that happiness (beatitudo) consists in activity. He thus defined the nature of this activity: 'Happiness consists in fruition, that is, in the love of the beloved object for its own sake.'[4] Incidentally, Henry of Ghent, the *Doctor Solemnis*, anticipated the teachings of Duns Scotus. Henry taught that love is a higher activity than wisdom, and that the will (of which love is the *habitus*), is more perfectly united with its object than the intellect.

The difference of outlook was a natural outcome of the character of the two organizations. St. Dominic aspired to imitate the outer mission of Christ, St. Francis to imitate His poverty and humility. The Dominicans were to teach both by word and deed, the Franciscans by practice rather than by precept. The former were fittingly known as the Order of Preachers, the latter endeavoured to show forth in their lives the Divine Love. St. Dominic strove to heal the wounds of the world by the appeal to reason, St. Francis by the appeal to the heart. It was natural that the Minorities should feel attracted by Neo-Platonism, as modified by Augustine, in whose theology the love of God plays such a large part. It was equally natural that the Friars Preachers should find in Aristotle, as he was then understood, a congenial guide. It is typical that the word *Erkenntnis* (knowledge, cognition) should often be on the lips of the German Dominicans,

---

[1] *Itinerarium Mentis ad Deum*, cap. V, 8.
[2] As does Preger, *Geschichte*, II, p. 89, though with some reservations.
[3] John xvii. 3. [4] *Sententiarum*, Lib. IV, Dist. XLIX, Quaest. 1, 5.

whereas the Franciscans laid more stress on *Minne* (love). Suso is a notable exception to the general rule.

The antagonism between intellect and emotion finds an echo in an anonymous treatise edited by Pfeiffer.[1] It is the work of a Franciscan, a contemporary of the sermon writer discussed above. He mentions the dispute among the masters whether blessedness was more a question of love or of knowledge. He gives the preference to love, because love follows knowledge (we cannot love what we do not know), and love unites more than knowledge. Knowledge is satisfied with an image of the thing known; love is not content with any image, but wishes to be completely united with the thing loved. Another treatise by the same writer deals with mystical problems: the birth of the Word in the soul; the love of man for God; the manner in which the blessed know God; what constitutes perfect knowledge; and finally, the love which the blessed feel for God in heaven.

Enough has been said to show that up to the early fourteenth century the German Franciscans had an active intellectual life, and some of them at least had mystical proclivities. With the untimely death of Duns Scotus in 1308, within a year of his installation at Cologne, scholarship suffered a heavy blow. There were other difficulties for the German Minorites. The quarrels about poverty, and the persecution of the *Fraticelli*, or Spirituals, consumed a good deal of their energy. This unfortunate cleavage began in the first half of the thirteenth century, and it was widened after 1274. Further, the life of the Franciscans was less secluded than that of the Dominicans, some of whom, as we have seen, were allowed to concentrate on learning and contemplation. The religious life of the Minorites in Germany at this time was practical in character; it was more productive of good works than of good literature.

After 1330 things were different: the *Fraticelli* ceased to be a decisive factor. There was still a severance, but it took a milder form and was limited to single friaries. The Observantines or Friars of the Strict Observance came to be separated from the Conventuals and a *modus vivendi* was found. The hostility between the two great Mendicant Orders which was so painfully evident at Eckhart's trial had largely subsided. The strife between the Pope and the Emperor was at an end. Between 1340 and 1350 there was a revival of Franciscan mysticism.

Among the best-known works written at this time is *The Book of*

---

[1] In *Zeitschrift für deutsches Alterthum*, VIII (1851), p. 422 sqq.

Spiritual Poverty. It also went by the name of *The Imitation of the Poor Life of Christ*, and was attributed by its editor, Sudermann,[1] to Tauler. It was the merit of Denifle to prove conclusively that Tauler was not the author.[2] Neither in style nor in subject-matter has the work anything in common with Tauler's writings. The author asserts that all men are called to outer poverty. The highest perfection consists in possessing nothing at all. Those riches in worldly goods are the biggest rogues. The true Friend of God is to be detected by this 'means test.' Tauler never makes such an assertion. He stresses internal poverty. In his view, only conventuals are required to give up all their possessions, or such persons to whom wealth is a cause of stumbling, like the young man in Scripture. To make wise provision for the future is not necessarily sinful. Tauler says that different persons are called to different kinds of lives, and not all are called upon to embrace poverty.

Some of the remarks of the unknown author border on quietism. He maintains that if a man wishes to come to God he must divest himself of outer works, even works of love, and must become entirely passive. But in his efforts to avoid extreme quietism, the writer becomes inconsistent and contradicts himself. The emphasis on poverty as almost a virtue in itself is typically Franciscan and finds its most uncompromising formulation among the *Fraticelli*, who made it an article of faith to put the Rule of St. Francis into literal practice. Denifle therefore ascribes the work to a moderate Spiritual Minorite. The whole attitude is that of the Franciscans and some of the teachings recall those of Duns Scotus. There are parallels to Eckhart and Tauler, but no sign of direct influence. The author (or authors) deals *inter alia* with the birth of God in the soul, the word spoken by God in the soul. He is a mystic and a Friend of God, but not a theologian. The approximate date of the work is 1350. That it is in the direct line of Franciscan tradition is indicated by the fact that it is quoted several times by Marquart von Lindau.

At first the Clarisses, or Franciscan nuns, were subject to the Benedictine Rule, but by degrees a *rapprochement* to the Minorites took place, partly because both friars and sisters revered a common founder and partly because the Clarisses were enabled by this means to benefit by the papal privileges given to the Friars Minor. In 1245

---

[1] Frankfort, 1621.

[2] Further arguments were brought forward by Ritschl, *Untersuchung des Buches Von geistlicher Armut*, who showed that it is a heterogeneous composition, consisting of several different treatises.

Innocent IV placed things on a legal basis and entrusted to the Minorites the entire spiritual care of all convents of Clarisses.

This duty proved no less irksome for the Franciscans than it had been for the Dominicans. The frequent visits to nunneries, the preaching of sermons and hearing of confessions, the selection or composition of devotional literature, occupied a great deal of time and interfered with learned pursuits. The effects on scholarship could not fail to be harmful. It was the very friars who were engaged in teaching and writing who were responsible for the *cura monalium*.

Yet we hear very little about the religious lives of these Franciscan nuns. In Dominican convents the *Lives* of sisters who had visions or ecstasies, and the personal records of mystical experiences are numerous. At Freiburg in Breisgau the biographies of no less than thirty-six nuns were written about 1318.[1] At Engeltal Christina Ebner recorded information about the lives of fifty inmates of her convent. Elsbeth Stagel narrates the lives of thirty sisters at Töss. There is no parallel to this in the annals of the Franciscan nunneries of Germany. None of the Clarisses attained the fame of Christina and Margareta Ebner or Elsbeth Stagel. There are just stray references to mystical experiences in Franciscan nunneries, for instance at Wittichen in the Black Forest.[2]

One friar who was a confessor of Clarisses is known to us by name. Claus, or Nicolaus, von Blaufelden, was a native of a village in Würtemberg. About the year 1379 he wrote to Grüner Wörth in Strasbourg, that famous workshop for the manufacture and distribution of ascetic literature, asking for some suitable reading matter for his charges. He received a tractate entitled *Der Schürebrand*.[3] The author seems to have been one of the Knights of St. John rather than Rulman Merswin, although there are some reminiscences of the latter's prolix style, with its *clichés* and frequent repetitions.

Friar Claus revised the manuscript, introducing the names of St. Francis and St. Clare wherever necessary, and adding three rules for the conduct of life for nuns. The little book instructs the sisters to be assiduous in their religious duties, to sing the office joyfully, for if they cannot understand the words, God and His angels understand them. There are numerous references to the Friends of God. Among saints and enlightened teachers the author mentions St. Augustine, St. Jerome, St. Ambrose, and St. Bernard, and finally Tauler, Suso 'and many like them.' But there is no trace of anything that could

---

[1] Preger, *Geschichte*, I, 138.   [2] Preger, II, p. 257.
[3] Edited by Strauch, *Studien zur deutschen Philologie*, Halle, 1903.

properly be called mysticism in the work. It is interesting as indicating that at this time the great Dominican mystics were regarded as worthy models to be followed in Franciscan friaries and nunneries.

One can have no hestitation in numbering Marquart (or Marcus, this being the Latinized form of his name) von Lindau among the mystics. He studied at the University of Basel and took his doctorate there in 1379. After administering the custody of Lacus or Bodensee (Lake Constance), he was elected Provincial Minister of Upper Germany in 1389. He died at Constance in 1392. For a time he was a scribe in the Tyrol, probably in the Abbey of Stams. In the library of Innsbruck there are manuscripts copied by his hand.[1] Leopold of Austria held sway at Basel in 1379 when Marquart resided in that city. He then belonged to the party of the Avignon Pope. In 1392, in Strasbourg, he was of the Roman obedience. This somewhat unusual change of allegiance, which rather reminds us of the Vicar of Bray, might indicate that Marquart was a peace-loving man and not very much interested in politics, though some would find a harsher name for it.

The Franciscan historian Glassberger enumerates twenty-nine books written by Marquart von Lindau. There are his sermons, five of which are bound together with some of Tauler's works. Then there are a number of treatises in Latin and German on a variety of theological topics. Many of them are quite short, all are characterized by simplicity, clarity and popular tone. His exposition of the Creed is an admirably concise statement of the essentials of the Christian faith. Marquart's fame chiefly rests on an account of the Exodus of the Children of Israel. This work, which is in German, is in the form of a dialogue between master and pupil and is evidently meant for nuns. In spite of his not inconsiderable learning, Marquart is an eminently practical person. He excels in pointing out the application and the relevance of a biblical story to the daily needs of his readers.

I have shown elsewhere that Marquart quotes Eckhart and Tauler in his *Exodus*.[2] In his *Commentary on the Gospel of St. John* he borrows largely from Eckhart's work on the same subject. We find imbedded in his writings some of the most beautiful passages of these great mystics. Neither of them is named; in the case of Eckhart this is natural enough, nor need we be surprised at the omission of Tauler's

---

[1] E.g. University Library, No. 627. An inscription in this codex shows that Marquart had the cognomen 'Toder' or 'the Stammerer.'

[2] *Modern Language Review*, Vol. XXXIV (1939), pp. 73–78; see also Vol. XLII (1947), pp. 246–251.

*

name. It is common mediaeval practice only to mention by name those authors who were of unquestionable authority, such as the Fathers of the Church or the founders of Scholasticism.

A commentary on the Bible does not give much scope for originality, but Marquart's work has some special features. There is, for example, a lengthy digression about the ideas.[1] Though in part a loose paraphrase of Augustine[2] and Thomas Aquinas,[3] this passage goes far beyond the general teachings of these writers. The ideas are for Marquart not only the prototypes of everything on earth, the source of all human knowledge (here we get the Platonic doctrine) and the happiness of the saints in heaven, they are also the cause (sach, Ursache) of the creatures in this world, 'Some say: "This hand created heaven and earth," and they are right, if they mean the idea of the hand, which is part of God.' They (the ideas) are 'flowing rivers of divine sweetness. Let us imbibe therefrom divine wisdom.' Past and future are both present in the ideas. The Antichrist and the end of the world are both visible as in a mirror. In Eckhart's *Commentary* there are brief passages on the subject, but Eckhart always uses the phrase *rationes rerum*, whereas Marquart uses *ydeas* or *formae ydeales*;[4] hence direct borrowing is unlikely here. The reader will remember that Eckhart indignantly denied having said that his little finger had created the world, which is the kind of thing that Marquart is here saying.

In his attitude to the old controversy between Dominicans and Franciscans as to the relative merits of will and knowledge, Marquart shows himself to be a Scotist rather than a Thomist. He places the will above cognition (Erkenntnis).[5] Lucifer, he tells us, has knowledge, but is in hell, because he lacks the will. Martyrs are superior to confessors, because the will is higher than knowledge. The will 'penetrates the unity of the highest will and the power of love and becomes one with the pure and only Good, eternally united.' Here we have the unmistakable mystical touch. On the question of the immanence of God, he keeps to the strictly orthodox line and quotes Thomas Aquinas: God is in everything *per essentiam, per potentiam, per praesentiam*, by His essence or nature as Creator, by His power as Upholder, by His presence as Judge of all actions.[6]

At the time when Marquart wrote, the great creative period of

---

[1] Innsbruck, University Library, MS. No. 627, fol. 40r–42v.
[2] *De Divinis Quaestionibus* (Migne, *Patriologia Latina*, t. 40, col. 30).
[3] *Summa Theologica*, I, Quaest. XIV; Quaest. XV, Art. 1, 3.
[4] He translates this 'formliche pild.'   [5] *Munich*, Cgm. No. 506, fo. 121v.
[6] *Innsbruck*, No. 627, fo. 95r–96r.

German mysticism was over. We find few original ideas in him, his mysticism is entirely Dominican, except for the influence of Duns Scotus and Bonaventura. His function is to preserve a dying tradition from complete extinction rather than to produce something new. The rest of the story can be told briefly. There are fragments of other Franciscan mystical works: a sermon by Friar Volmar and a few quotations from another friar of the same name who may or may not be the same person. There is a sermon by a certain Friar Alhart, of whom nothing further has been discovered. Otto von Passau represents the final phase.

He was a lector in the Franciscan friary at Basel in 1362 and guardian in the following year. He died after 1385, in which year he is mentioned as a member of the Basel chapter. His voluminous work *Die zweiundzwanzig Alten* or *Der goldene Thron der minnenden Seele* received its final form in 1386. The title is taken from the Apocalypse. Each of the twenty-four Elders holds forth on some devotional topic, such as contrition, penance, Holy Communion, love of God and one's neighbour and so on. A hundred and four authors are quoted with a connecting link between, so the book is really a string of long quotations. The general theme is the conduct needful to attain eternal life. Otto is a compiler, not an original author. Over one hundred manuscripts of the work are in existence, chiefly in South German libraries. It continued to enjoy great popularity till after the Reformation.

One chapter only, the sixteenth, is mystical in theme, since it is concerned with the contemplative life, the stages of purification by which the soul ascends to the beatific vision. Otto is careful to say that no one can attain true contemplation unless he has first practised good works. It is for this reason that he prefixes to this section one on the active life, thus settling in the orthodox sense a problem that exercised the spirits of the *Gottesfreunde* very deeply. But we cannot call Otto von Passau a mystic in the full sense of the word. He can describe phenomena, classify experiences, but he is a writer about the inner religious life rather than one who is telling what he himself has seen and felt. He lacks originality and his style is heavy and formal. He leaves us in no doubt as to his public. His book is intended for 'all Friends of God, spiritual and lay, noble and simple, men and women.'

SELECT BIBLIOGRAPHY

I. ECKHART

(i) Editions

Bascour, H., *Magistri Eckardi Opera Latina*. II *Opus Tripartitum: Prologi*, Lipsiae, 1935.

Birlinger, A., 'Tractate Meister Eckharts,' *Alemannia*, iii, 1875.

Daniels, A., 'Eine lateinische Rechtfertigungsschrift des Meister Eckhart,' BBG, xxiii, Heft 5, 1923. Edition of documents of trial at Cologne.

Denifle, H. S., 'Actenstücke zu Meister Eckharts Process,' ZfdA, xxix, 1885.

Denifle, H. S., 'Meister Eckeharts lateinische Schriften und die Grundanschauung seiner Lehre,' ALKM, ii, 1886. First edition of the Latin works with valuable commentary.

Diederichs, E., 'Meister Eckharts Reden der Unterscheidung,' KT, No. 117, 1913.

Dondaine, A., *Magistri Eckardi Opera Latina*. XIII *Quaestiones*, Lipsiae, 1936.

Geyer, B., *Quaestiones et Sermo Parisiensis*, Bonnae, 1931.

Jostes, F., *Meister Eckehart und seine Jünger. Ungedruckte Texte zur Geschichte der deutschen Mystik*, Freiburg (Schweiz), 1895. Very important source.

Jundt, A., *Histoire du panthéisme populaire au moyen âge*, Paris, 1875. Texts attributed to Eckhart and Merswin.

Klibansky, R., *Magistri Eckhardi Opera Latina*. I. *Super Oratione Dominica*, Lipsiae, 1934.

Langenberg, R., *Quellen und Forschungen zur Geschichte der deutschen Mystik*, Bonn, 1902. Text of Low German sermons.

Longpré, E., 'Questions inédites de Maître Eckahrt, O.P. et de Gonzalve de Balboa, O.F.M.,' *Revue néo-scholastique*, 1927.

Pahncke, M., 'Zwei ungedruckte Mystikerreden,' Zfda, xlix, 1908.

Pelster, F., 'Ein Gutachten aus dem Eckhart-Prozess in Avignon,' Supplementband III, 1. Halbband, 1935. Documents of the Avignon trial.

Pfeiffer, F., *Meister Eckhart*, 4th edition, Göttingen, 1924. Standard edition of the German works. To be used with caution.

Preger, W., *Geschichte der deutschen Mystik im Mittelhalter*, 3 vols., Leipzig, 1874, 1881, 1893. A survey of the whole field.

Preger, W., 'Meister Eckhart und die Inquisition,' *Abhandlungen der Bayerischen Akademie*, Bd. xi, Abt. 2, 1869. First edition of trial documents.

Quint, J., 'Eine unbekannte echte Predigt Meister Eckeharts,' ZfdP, lx, 1935.

Schönbach, A. E., 'Altdeutsche Funde aus Innsbruck,' ZfdA, xxxv, 1891.

Sievers, E., 'Predigten von Meister Eckart,' ZfdA, xv, 1872. Text of sermons from Oxford (Laud) and Cassel MSS.

Spamer, A., *Texte aus der Mystik des 14. und 15. Jahrhunderts*, Jena, 1912.

Strauch, P., 'Buch der geistlichen Tröstung und von dem edlen Menschen (Liber Benedictus),' KT, No. 55, 1910. Standard edition.

Strauch, P., 'Paradisus Anime Intelligentis,' *Deutsche Texte des Mittelalters*, xxx, 1919. Collection of mystical sermons.

Strauch, P., 'Zur Überlieferung Meister Eckharts,' PBB, xlix, 1925. Ten sermons from a Berlin MS.

Théry, G., 'Edition critique des pièces relatives au procès d'Eckhart contenues dans le manuscrit 33b de la bibliothèque de Soest,' AHDL, 1926. Best edition of documents of trial.

Théry, G., 'Le Commentaire de Maître Eckhart sur le livre de la Sagesse,' AHDL, 1929. Edition with valuable notes.

Weiss, K., Quint, J., Christ, K., Koch, J., *Meister Eckhart. Die deutschen und lateinischen Werke*, Stuttgart und Berlin, 1936–8.

(ii) Modernized Editions and Translations

Bernhart, J., *Meister Eckhart. Ausgewählt und übersetzt*, München 1914. Selection from sermons and tractates.

Büttner, H., *Meister Eckeharts Schriften und Predigten*, 2 vols., Jena, 1903. Popular edition with introduction.

Evans, C. de B., *Meister Eckhart. Translation*, London, 1924. Translation of Pfeiffer's edition with a few omissions.

Landauer, G., *Meister Eckharts mystische Schriften in unsere Sprache übertragen*, Berlin, 1903.

Lehmann, W., *Meister Eckhart*, Göttingen, 1919.

(iii) Literary Criticism

Bach, J., *Meister Eckhart, der Vater der deutschen Speculation*, Wien, 1864. One of the leading authorities of early period.

Boehmer, H., 'Loyola und die deutsche Mystik,' *Berichte der sächsischen Akademie*, lxxiii, 1921. Important article.

Bolza, O., *Meister Eckhart als Mystiker. Eine religionsgeschichtliche Studie*, München, 1938. Answers the question: Was E. himself a mystic?

Bracken, E. von, *Meister Eckhart und Fichte*, Würzburg, 1943. Voluminous work, but meagre conclusions.

Brethauer, K., 'Magistri Eckardi Opera Latina,' ZfdA, lxxxv, 1938.

Delacroix, H., *Essai sur le mysticisme spéculatif en Allemagne au quatorzième siècle*, Paris, 1900. One of leading French authorities.

Dempf, A., *Meister Eckhart. Eine Einführung in sein Werk*, Leipzig, 1934. Important contribution. Stress laid on the paradoxical element in E.'s philosophy.

Denifle, H. S., 'Die Heimat Meister Eckeharts,' ALKM, v, 1889.

Deutsch, S. M., 'Eckhart,' *Realencyclopädie für protestantische Theologie und Kirche*, v, 1898.

Diederichs, E., *Meister Eckharts Reden der Unterscheidung. Eine literarkritische Untersuchung*, Diss. Halle, 1912. Proves this treatise to be genuine.

Ebeling, H., *Meister Eckharts Mystik. Studien zu den Geisteskämpfen um die Wende des* 13. *Jahrhunderts*, Stuttgart, 1941. Learned philosophical work.

Grabmann, M., 'Neue Eckhartsforschungen im Lichte neuer Eckharts-funde,' *Divus Thomas*, v, 1927. Criticism of Karrer.

Grundmann, H., 'Meister Eckhart etwa 1260–1327,' *Die Grossen Deutschen. Neue deutsche Biographien*, i, 1935. Careful and concise survey of E.'s life and doctrines.

Haacke, M., *Der Gottesgedanke und das Gotteserlebnis bei Eckehart*, Diss. Greifswald, 1918. Systematic account of E.'s theology.

Hornstein, X. de, *Les grands mystiques allemands du xivᵉ siècle. Etat present des problèmes*, Lucerne, 1922.

Jundt, A., *Essai sur le mysticisme populaire de Maître Eckhart*, Strasbourg, 1871.

Karrer, O., *Das Göttliche in der Seele*, Würzburg, 1928.

Karrer, O., *Meister Eckhart. Das System seiner religiösen Lehre und seiner Lebensweisheit*, München, 1926. Mass of quotations and references systematically arranged.

Koch, J., 'Meister Eckhart,' Die Kirche in der Zeitwende, Paderborn, 1935. Contemporary opinions about E.

Lasson, A., *Meister Eckehart der Mystiker*, Berlin, 1868. One of best early authorities.

Lasson, A., Quint, J., 'Eckhart,' *Grundriss der Geschichte der Philosophie*, 2. Teil, 1928. Philosophical investigation of E.

Lehmann, W., *Meister Eckehart, der gotische Mystiker*, Lübeck, 1933. Very good account of life and writings.

Linsenmann, F. X., *Der ethische Charakter der Lehre Meister Eckharts*, Tübingen, 1873. A sympathetic approach.

Martensen, H. L., *Meister Eckart. Eine theologische Studie*, Hamburg, 1842.

Otto, R., *West-Östliche Mystik*, Gotha, 1926. A comparison of E. with Hindu mystics. English translation by B. L. Bracey and R. C. Payne, 1932.

Pahncke, M., 'Ein Grundgedanke der deutschen Predigt Meister Ecke-harts,' ZfKG, xxxiv, 1913.

Pahncke, M., 'Meister Eckeharts Lehre von der Geburt Gottes im Gerech-ten,' *Archiv für Religionswissenschaft*, xxiii, 1925.

Piesch, H., *Meister Eckharts Ethik*, Luzern, 1925. Apologia of E. by learned orthodox Catholic.

Piesch, H., 'Meister Eckhart heute,' *Zeitschrift für deutsche Geistesgeschichte*, iii, 1937. Excellent survey of recent publications.

Pummerer, A., 'Der gegenwärtige Stand der Eckhart-Forschung,' *Jahresbericht, Gymnasium,* Feldkirch, 1903. Careful examination of all documents referring to E.'s life.

Quint, J., 'Die gegenwärtige Problemstellung der Eckhartforschung,' ZfdP, lii, 1927. Important survey of E. scholarship.

Quint, J., 'Meister Eckehart,' *Von deutscher Art und Dichtung,* iii, 1941. Diffusion of MSS. in Germany; facts about E.'s life.

Seeberg, E., *Meister Eckhart,* Tübingen, 1934.

Vernet, F., 'Eckart,' *Dictionnaire de Théologie Catholique,* iv, 1924. One of the best French contributions.

Wenck, J., 'Ignotae Litteraturae,' BGPM, vii, Heft 6, 1910.

(iv) Philological Criticism

Behaghel, O., 'Zur Kritik von Meister Eckhart,' PBB, xxxiv, 1909.

Denifle, H. S., 'Zu Meister Eckhart,' ZfdA, xxi, 1877. New MSS. of Swester Katrei and other works.

Emunds, H., *Meister Eckharts Predigt*: 'Vff Sant Dominicustag,' Diss. Bonn, 1924.

Eucken, R., *Geschichte der philosophischen Terminologie,* Leipzig, 1879. Important.

Hammerich, L. L., 'Das Trostbuch Meister Eckeharts,' ZfdP, lvi, 1931. Textual criticism of Trostbuch and sermon Vom edlen Menschen; investigation of date, place, etc.

Kramm, E., 'Meister Eckharts Terminologie,' ZfdP, xvi, 1884.

Kunisch, H., 'Theophora Schneider, Der intellektuelle Wortschatz Meister Eckharts,' ZfdA, lv, 1936. Searching criticism of this article and of technique of 'Feldforschung.'

Lotze, A., *Kritische Beiträge zu Meister Eckhart,* Diss. Halle, 1907. Materials for new critical edition of E.

Müller, G., 'Zur Überlieferung Taulers und Eckharts,' ZfdA, lxi, 1924.

Pahncke, M., 'J. Quint, Die Überlieferung der deutschen Predigten Meister Eckeharts,' ZfdP, lx, 1935. Survey of textual criticism of Pfeiffer; additions to Quint's observations.

Pahncke, M., 'Materialien zu Meister Eckeharts Predigt über die Armut des Geistes,' *Hermaea,* xxxi, 1932. Deals with No. 87 in Pfeiffer.

Pahncke, M., *Untersuchungen zu den deutschen Predigten Meister Eckharts,* Diss. Halle, 1905.

Quint, J., *Meister Eckhart. Die deutschen und lateinischen Werke.* 1. Band. *Untersuchungen,* Stuttgart und Berlin, 1940. Very important contribution; 89 new MSS. of E. and other mystics described in detail.

Quint, J., 'Die Sprache Meister Eckeharts als Ausdruck seiner mystischen Geisteswelt,' DVLG, vi, 1928.

Quint, J., *Die Überlieferung der Deutschen Predigten Meister Eckeharts,* Bonn, 1932. Critical examination of all sermons in Pfeiffer. Most important.

Schneider, Th., 'Der intellektuelle Wortschatz Meister Eckeharts,' *Neue Deutsche Forschungen. Abteilung Deutsche Philologie*, xiv, 1935. Survey of E.'s abstract vocabulary from standpoint of 'Feldforschung.'

Skutella, F., 'Beiträge zur kritischen Ausgabe deutscher Predigten M. Eckharts,' ZfdA, lxviii, 1931. Methods of testing genuineness, and summary of results thus obtained.

Spamer, A., 'Zur Überlieferung der Pfeifferschen Eckeharttexte,' PBB, xxxiv, 1909.

Zuchhold, H., 'Des Nikolaus von Landau Sermone als Quelle für die Predigt Meister Eckharts und seines Kreises,' *Hermaea*, ii, 1905.

II. TAULER, SUSO AND OTHER MYSTICS

(i) Editions

Bihlmeyer, K., *Heinrich Seuse, Deutsche Schriften*, Stuttgart, 1907. Standard edition with excellent notes and introduction.

Corin, A. L., 'Sermons de J. Tauler et autres écrits mystiques,' *Bibliothèque de la Faculté de Philosophie et Lettres*, Liège, xxxiii, xlii, 1924, 1929. Some new sermons from Vienna MSS.

Denifle, H. S., *Das Buch von geistlicher Armut, bisher bekannt als Johann Taulers Nachfolgung des armen Lebens Christi*, München, 1877. Not by Tauler; author unknown.

Jundt, A., *Histoire du panthéisme populaire au moyen âge*, Paris 1875. Edition of Merswin's Buch von den drei Durchbrüchen and Bannerbüchlein, and of two sermons by Eckhart.

Jundt, A., *Les Amis de Dieu au quatorzième siècle*, Paris, 1879.

Naumann, L., 'Ausgewählte Predigten Johann Taulers,' KT, No. 127, 1914. 8 sermons from MSS. and early printed editions.

Priebsch, R., 'Aus deutschen Handschriften der kgl. Bibliothek zu Brüssel,' ZfdP, xxxvi, 1904. Sermons by Suso; fragments attributed to Eckhart and Tauler.

Schmidt, C., *Bericht von der Bekehrung Taulers*, Strassburg, 1875. The spurious life of T. with two sermons.

Schmidt, K., *Nicolaus von Basel Leben und ausgewählte Schriften*, Wien, 1866. Important.

Strauch, P., 'Schürebrand, ein Traktat aus dem Kreise der Strassburger Gottesfreunde,' *Studien zur deutschen Philologie*, 1903. Excellent edition with glossary and introduction.

Strauch, P., Margaretha Ebner und Heinrich von Nördlingen, Freiburg i.B und Tübingen, 1882. Critical edition of correspondence.

Strauch, P., 'Schriften aus der Gottesfreundliteratur,' *Altdeutsche Textbibliothek*, Nos. 22, 23, 27, Halle, 1927. Text of 7 treatises by Merswin.

Vetter, F., 'Die Predigten Taulers,' *Deutsche Texte des Mittelalters*, xi, 1910.

Wackernagel, W., *Altdeutsche Predigten und Gebete*, Basel, 1876. Texts and criticism.

(ii) Translations and Modernized Editions

Denifle, H. S., *Deutsche Schriften des sel. Heinrich Seuse*, München, 1876.
Diepenbrock, M., *Heinrich Suso's, genannt Amandus, Leben und Schriften*, 3rd ed., Regensburg, 1884.
Gabele, A., *Deutsche Schriften von Heinrich Seuse*, Leipzig, 1924.
Greiner, M., *Heinrich Seuse, Das Büchlein der Ewigen Weisheit*, Leipzig, 1935. Selections only, with short introduction.
Hugueny, Théry and Corin, A. L., *Sermons de Tauler*, Paris, 1928. With full literary and theological introductions and life of T.
Lavaud, B., *Henri Suso, L'Oeuvre mystique*, Paris, 1946. A new French translation with notes and introduction.
Naumann, L., *Johann Tauler, Predigten*, Leipzig, 1923. Selection.
Oehl, W., *Tauler*, München, 1919. 19 sermons translated with excellent introduction; semi-popular.
Thiriot, G., *Oeuvres mystiques du Bienheureux Henri Suso*, 2 vols., Paris, 1899. Based on Denifle's text, includes the letters.
Winkworth, S., *The History and Life of the Rev. Dr. John Tauler of Strasbourg*, London, 1857.
    There are English translations of Suso's *Little Book of Eternal Wisdom* by F. M. M. Comper (1910), T. F. Knox (1913), R. Raby (1852) and C. H. McKenna, New York (1889).

(iii) Literary Criticism

Baehring, B., *Johann Tauler und die Gottesfreunde*, Hamburg, 1853.
Bihlmeyer, K., 'Des schwäbischen Mystikers Heinrich Seuse Abstammung und Geburt,' HPB, cxxx, 1, Heft, 1902.
Bühlmann, J., *Christuslehre und Christusmystik des Heinrich Seuse*, Luzern, 1942. Examination of S's style and influence on devotion.
Chiquot, A., *Histoire ou légende? Jean Tauler et le 'Meisters buoch,'* Strasbourg et Paris, 1922. The Life a forgery.
Denifle, H. S., 'Der Gottesfreund im Oberlande und Nikolaus von Basel,' HPB, lxxv, 1875. Nikolaus von Basel was not the Gottesfreund.
Denifle, H. S., 'Die Dichtungen des Gottesfreundes im Oberlande,' ZfdA, xxiv, 1880. The Life of Tauler and Rome journey of Gottesfreund are fictitious.
Denifle, H. S., 'Die Dichtungen Rulman Merswins,' ibid. The Gottesfreund an invention of Merswin.
Denifle, H. S., 'Taulers Bekehrung kritisch untersucht,' *Quellen und Forschungen zur Sprach- und Kulturgeschichte*, xxxvi, 1879.
Grisar, H., *Luther*, Freiburg i. B., 1941. Luther's debt to Tauler.
Gröber, C., *Der Mystiker Heinrich Seuse*, Freiburg i.B., 1941. Careful survey of life and works, supporting authenticity of Life.

Hahn, S., 'Heinrich Susos Bedeutung als Philosoph,' BGPM, Supplementband, 1913. Short but sound.

Heieck, L., *Das Verhältnis des Ästhetischen zum Mystischen dargestellt an Heinrich Seuse*, Diss. Erlangen, 1936. S.'s style.

Jundt, A., *Rulman Merswin et l'ami de Dieu de l'Oberland. Un problème de psychologie religieuse*, Paris, 1890.

Kärcher, L., 'Heinrich Suso aus dem Predigerorden. Abhandlung über Ort und Zeit seiner Geburt,' *Freiburger Diöcesanarchiv*, iii, 1868.

Korn, A., *Tauler als Redner*, Münster i. W., 1928.

Köstlin, J., *Luthers Theologie in ihrer geschichtlichen Entwicklung dargestellt*, Stuttgart, 1863. Detailed treatment of Tauler's influence on Luther.

Lichtenberger, H., 'Le mystique Suso,' *Revue des Cours et Conferences*, xviii, xx, 1909–11. Best account in French. Life not authentic.

Müller, G., 'Scholastikerzitate bei Tauler,' DVLG, i, 1923. Scholastic influences in T.

Preger, W., 'Die Zeit einiger Predigten Taulers,' *Sitzungsberichte der Akademie der Wissenschaften*, München, 1887, 2. Band.

Rieder, C., *Der Gottesfreund vom Oberland*, Innsbruck, 1905. Not Merswin, but Nikolaus von Löwen, was the inventor of the Gottesfreund.

Rieder, K., 'Karl Bihlmeyer, Heinrich Seuse,' *Göttingische Gelehrte Anzeigen*, clxxi, 2. Band, 1909. Suso's Life spurious.

Ritschl, A., 'Untersuchungen des Buches Von geistlicher Armut,' ZfKG, iv, 1881. Not by Tauler.

Schmidt, C., 'Der Mystiker Heinrich Suso,' TSK, vi, 1843. Important, though superseded in details.

Schmidt, C., *Johannes Tauler von Strassburg*, Hamburg, 1841. With supplement on the Friends of God.

Senn, R., *Die Echtheit der Vita Heinrich Seuses*, Bern, 1930. Genuineness of Life upheld.

Siedel, G., *Die Mystik Taulers*, Leipzig, 1911.

Seitz, J., *Der Traktat des 'Unbekannten deutschen Mystikers' bei Greith*, Diss. Zürich, 1936. Not original, but compiled from Eckhart, Tauler, Dionysius, etc.

Stöckerl, D., *Bruder David von Augsburg. Ein deutscher Mystiker aus dem Franziskanerorden*, München, 1914. Sound work.

Strauch, P., 'Der Gottesfreund vom Oberland eine Erfindung des Strassburger Johanniters Nikolaus von Löwen,' ZfdP, xxxix, 1907. Rejects Rieder's conclusions. Careful research.

Thimme, W., Über Verfasserschaft und Zuverlässigkeit der Vita H. Seuses,' TSK, ciii, 1931. Exhaustive treatment. The Vita is genuine.

Vetter, F., *Ein Mystikerpaar des vierzehnten Jahrhunderts. Schwester Elsbeth Stagel in Töss und Vater Amandus* (Suso) *in Konstanz*, Basel, 1882. Charming study of two mystics.

Weymann, U., *Die Seusesche Mystik und ihre Wirkung auf die bildende Kunst*, Berlin, 1938.

(iv) Philological Criticism

Beck, J. J., *De Johannes Taulerii Ord. Praed. Dictione Vernacula et Mystica*, Argentorati, 1786.

Corin, A. L., 'Zur Filiation der Taulerischen Handschriften,' *Revue belge de philosophie et d'histoire*, iii, 1924.

Denifle, H. S., 'Zu Seuses ursprünglichem Briefbuch,' ZfdA, xix, 1876.

Naumann, L., 'Die Wiener Taulerhandschriften 2739 und 2744,' ZfdP, xlvi, 1876.

Naumann, L., *Untersuchungen zu Johann Taulers Deutschen Predigten*, Diss. Rostock, 1911.

Nicklas, A., *Die Terminologie des Mystikers Heinrich Seuse*, Königsberg i. P., 1914.

Peterson, E., 'Der Gottesfreund,' ZfkG, xlii, 1923.

Preger, W., 'Die Briefbücher Susos,' ZfdA, xv, 1876.

Strauch, P., 'Zu Taulers Predigten,' PBB, xliv, 1920. List of 89 Tauler MSS, critique of Vetter.

Vogt-Terhorst, A., 'Der bildliche Ausdruck in den Predigten Johann Taulers,' *Germanistische Abhandlungen*, lv, 1920.

Vulpinus, Th., 'Eine zweite Colmarer Suso-Handschrift,' *Jahrbuch für Geschichte, Sprache und Literatur Elsass-Lothringens*, XIX, 1903. A new MS. of *The Little Book of Eternal Wisdom*.

ABBREVIATIONS

AfdA	Anzeiger für deutsches Altertum.
ALKM	Archiv für die Literatur und Kirchengeschichte des Mittelalters.
AHDL	Archives d'histoire doctrinale et littéraire du moyen âge.
BBG	Bäumkers Beiträge zur Geschichte der Philosophie und Theologie des Mittelalters.
DVLG	Deutsche Vierteljahrsschrift für Literaturgeschichte und Geistesgeschichte.
HPB	Historisch-politische Blätter für das katholische Deutschland.
KT	Kleine Texte für theologische und philosophische Vorlesungen herausgegeben von Hanz Lietzmann.
PBB	Beiträge zur Geschichte der deutschen Sprache und Literatur.
TSK	Theologische Studien und Kritiken.
ZfdA	Zeitschrift für deutsches Altertum.
ZfdP	Zeitschrift für deutsche Philologie.
ZfKG	Zeitschrift für Kirchengeschichte.

INDEX